I Hear America Reading

Why We Read ⪜ What We Read

I HEAR AMERICA READING

WHY WE READ ⬙ WHAT WE READ

JIM BURKE

Foreword by

JOHN Y. COLE

DIRECTOR, THE CENTER FOR THE BOOK
LIBRARY OF CONGRESS

HEINEMANN
PORTSMOUTH, NH

Heinemann
A division of Reed Elsevier Inc.
361 Hanover Street
Portsmouth, NH 03801–3912
http://www.heinemann.com

Offices and agents throughout the world

Library of Congress Cataloging-in-Publication Data
I hear America reading : why we read, what we read / [compiled by] Jim Burke.
  p.   cm.
  ISBN 0-325-00134-0
  1. Books and reading—United States.   I. Burke, Jim, 1961– .
  Z1003.2.I34   1999   99-33312
  028'.9'0973—dc21   CIP

Editor: Lois Bridges
Production: Abigail M. Heim
Cover design: Joni Doherty Design
Cover photograph: Bates Hall Reading Room, Boston Public Library c. 1911, courtesy of the Boston Public Library, Print Dept. Photograph by N. L. Stebbins.
Manufacturing: Louise Richardson

Printed in the United States of America on acid-free paper
03 02 01 00   DA   3 4 5

To America's librarians and teachers

and to my students

They are not choosing the books over life outside. They are trying to persist against the obvious odds; they are asserting a common right to ask; they are attempting to find once again—among the ruins, in the astonished recognition that reading sometimes grants —an understanding.

—Alberto Manguel, from *A History of Reading*

I hungered for books, new ways of looking and seeing. It was not a matter of believing or disbelieving what I read, but of feeling something new, of being affected by something that made the look of the world different.

—Richard Wright, from *Black Boy*

Contents

Foreword

≈

The importance of particular books to particular individuals—to you and to me—often gets lost in today's whirling, digitized world. "You still think about *Captain from Castile?* You've got to be kidding!" is a response I've gotten from certain friends. Well, I've pretty much stopped sharing my formative reading experiences in public. Privately, however, my thoughts along these lines have intensified. Moreover, I'm worried about the future of reading in our country (OK, I admit I'm past my 55th birthday and grew up on Kenneth Roberts, Will Durant, Betty MacDonald and, somehow, John O'Hara).

Furthermore, I have professional reasons to be concerned. As director of the Center for the Book in the Library of Congress since it was established in 1977, I have seen our country's devotion to the printed word waver. The Center for the Book energetically uses television, radio, and even the Internet (check us out at http://lcweb.loc.gov/loc/cfbook) to promote books, reading, and libraries. We now have a network of 36 affiliated state centers and more than 50 national organizations as reading promotion partners. And still I worry.

This book, Jim Burke's *I Hear America Reading*, gives me hope. It contains dozens of heartening letters about personal reading experiences, illuminating "Why We Read" as well as "What We Read." These testimonials give us insight into both the intensity and the variety of personal reading experiences that shape individual lives. In my case, the letters remind me of the liberating (and yes, thrilling) experience that Samuel Shellabarger's *Captain from Castile* provided a certain teenager growing up in Bellingham, Washington, in the 1950s.

The reading experiences in this book give validity, in every sense, to the Center for the Book's motto: "Books Give Us Wings!"

John Y. Cole
Director, The Center for the Book
Library of Congress

Acknowledgments

From the moment the first letter arrived I understood I was being entrusted with something rare: the stories of people's lives. I am deeply grateful, as both the editor of this collection and the teacher who received them, to all who took time to write the letters that follow and, equally, those that ultimately were not chosen.

These letters on several occasions came close to being more than binders on my classroom shelves, but it took the commitment and interest of my editor and friend, Lois Bridges, to see them become a book.

The Library of Congress' Center for the Book showed an interest in these letters early on after someone wrote to tell the center about the letters. While the center could not find a use for the letters back then, I am grateful to its director, John Cole, whom I thank for his foreword and the resources he sent me.

I also wish to thank the following people for their help in locating correspondents, their contributions to the book lists in the appendix, or their assistance in preparing the manuscript:

Jacob Abrams, Dick Allington, Jan Bergamini, Hillary Bissell, Sandy Briggs, Peter Briggs, Ruby Burnstein, S. Campbell, Elaine Caret, Marilyn Carpenter, Fran Claggett, Bill Clawson, Judy Cunningham, David Doty, Angus Dunstan, Antoinette Dykman, Joan Dykman, Tony Fadale, Alan Farstrup, Jean Horton, Teri Hu, Sam Intrator, Carol Jago, Elaine Johnson, Carol

Jones, Joann Kersten, David and Margo Kipps, Linda Kroll, Suzanne Laughrea, Lisa Luedeke, Patti MacKenzie, Jane Meade-Roberts, Kimberly Mittler, Pete O'Neill, Leigh Peake, Doris Salter, Kathleen Toft, Christine Tripp, Megan Tucker, Kami Winding, Dan Wolter, Bill Youngblood, and many of my students.

I wish, finally, to acknowledge the librarians and teachers who, in letter after letter, were singled out for the difference they made in the emotional and intellectual lives of the writers. If, as someone once said, a library contains the soul of a society, ours is, despite tragic reductions, a rich soul, as evidenced by the stories in this book.

Introduction

⟳

Thou reader throbbest life and pride and love the same as I,
Therefore for thee the following chants.
　　　　　　　　　　—Walt Whitman, *Leaves of Grass*

This is not a book about reading as much as it is a story about our culture, our selves, and what we love: in this case, reading. As the poet Muriel Rukeyser wrote, "our lives are not made up of atoms; they are made of stories," and so it seems, for here we read not about people sitting still reading books, but children remembering weekly rituals that took them to the library, people who escaped wars and found themselves through books they discovered on their own or through people who told them to read.

Of course, not everyone shares this same love of books, though readers would argue books are a means by which a person can better know and appreciate whatever they do love. It was in response to my high school sophomores who claimed to "hate" reading, who found it a chore, a curse, that I wrote the letter to the editor that yielded the letters in this book.

Certainly I belong to a "nation of readers," yet it is a country I came to slowly. I never hated reading when I was growing up, but I remember my early struggles to live in imagined worlds others' minds created. Still, I never felt about reading as one of my students did:

> I am not reading [*The Adventures of Huckleberry Finn*]. I do not know the last chapter I read. That is not important because I do not understand this book because this book is jibberish. I will not read this book for that reason. I do not think that your help will help. I would be willing to try once again in English once we get off this book. I was working before we started reading this book. I think *Huck Finn* is a dumb book that doesn't teach me anything. I would rather read the dictionary. I would value it a lot more. It is also easier to understand since it is written in English.

Harsh words, yet they are what I wake to each day, for they form a challenge to my profession, demanding that I somehow explain why books matter, why students should want to read what the school district and state require. The truth, however, is that such an appreciation for reading is a frail accomplishment: I myself only read perhaps three books during high school.

But there *were* moments, powerful, even confusing ones. I remember picking up a copy of *Serpico*, a book about the New York police officer who refused to participate in corruption. My father had read it and left it lying around. To a fourteen-year-old, this book seemed a revelation: In Frank Serpico I had found a man who stood for something, and who cared so much about the quality of his foods that he would cross the city for a particular salami. I disappeared into this book only to emerge and read nothing again for perhaps a year.

During my junior year of high school I had another encounter, one that still moves me. Despite being very ill, I went down to school to take the SAT; friends picked me up early that morning. I believe I got sick twice en route from the parking lot to the cafeteria where the test was being given. Moments after the test began I left, seeking shelter under a tree outside Mr. Baxter's class where I was busy failing English. I woke hours later, very confused about where I was. Stumbling my way back to the cafeteria, I found everyone gone, the campus empty, and myself too weak to do anything. So I shuffled over to my locker and took out *Bless the Beasts and the Children* by Glendon Swarthout, returned to my shade—and read. When I looked up from the book it was late afternoon in the quiet suburbs of Sacramento; but I had been elsewhere, doing other things, with kids my own age whom I had only just met but already knew better than most of my "real" friends. It was such moments as these that Franz Kafka referred to when he said reading worked like an ax to break open the frozen sea within us. It would take me still a few more years—two to be precise—before I would begin to seek out books, search in them for clues to myself and life and the world. But by the time I walked the couple miles home that day, I was changed in ways it would take me years to understand.

Certainly all readers (or nonreaders) face such pivotal moments: Will their parents read nightly to them? Will they attend a day care program where a teacher reads to them every day? Or will they have an uncle or parent or neighbor who takes them to the library every Friday afternoon to stock up on books for the week? One thing seems to unite many of the readers in this book: the seemingly random moment when a teacher or librarian put the perfect book in their hand that set a fire of recognition and revelation in their mind, suddenly helping them to find their place among Ray Bradbury's People of the Book in *Fahrenheit 451*.

I Hear America Reading appears in the midst of what some have referred to as "the reading wars." The arguments of these wars, however, about *how* we read, rarely take into consideration the more fundamental question of *why* we read. They forget, for example, the importance of such elegant arguments as the ones two elementary school students offer here. "I like books because I can read them," explains second-grader Kyra. Books, as fourth-grader Liz points out, are "great for having an excuse for staying up late. 'Mom dad you want me to be smart so let me stay up in till 10:00 all I'll do is read.'" There are many other reasons we love reading, including C. S. Lewis' explanation that "we read to know we are not alone."

These letters reflect the complicated story of our country's cultural history, and anticipate the future as well, since each one answers in its own way a question the whole book implies: Why read? This book is indeed a meditation in many voices, a chorus really, about reading—why we do it, how we began doing it, who started us or changed us. It is a refreshing digression from the endless arguments about how children learn to read or what goes on when we read. We have become so obsessed with arguing the theory of reading that we too often neglect the reason we read in the first place.

My student's blunt honesty responding to *Huck Finn* challenges our love, though. His dismissal of a book he never tried to read in the first place would suggest to some that he is lacking in intelligence or ability; yet the truth is that this particular young man was identified as a GATE (Gifted and Talented Education) student early on. I hope that somewhere in these letters an answer surfaces to address his frustration, to challenge his own beliefs about reading and its value. It was, however, with such students in mind that I wrote the following letter to the editor of the *San Francisco Chronicle*:

Dear Editor:

In an era of decreasing commitment to literacy—how else to explain the failure of the state, for example, to adequately fund the libraries?—it is no surprise that most students, too, are bypassing books.

Instead they look elsewhere for information, for entertainment, for experiences. I would like to invite you to write to my high school students about your experiences with books, perhaps telling them what role books and literature have played in your life.

I would be just as interested in hearing from the 6-year-old about her favorite book as the 60-year-old whose life was changed by the reading of a book. Send your letters to me at Burlingame High School. Thank you, and keep reading.

It was late during Thanksgiving vacation when I wrote this letter. The gesture was so whimsical that I forgot I wrote it until I arrived at school the following Tuesday to find the first batch of what would total more than four- hundred letters. They kept coming day after day, and so we began reading as many as we could in my class. Soon letters began coming from other newspapers, other regions of the country; I realized people had sent my letter on to other publications, extended the invitation to other communities. In this way the letters became an evolving miracle, one that amazed all of us with each new letter from a different state or even, in the case of Helen Waterbury, another country (China).

My students, mostly sophomores that year, were visibly affected by this attention; they could not understand why so many people, from so many places, would take time to write to them about reading. In this respect the letters achieved some lasting change: students from that year still remember these letters; and in my own teaching I have learned to help students find the books that will speak to them and to convince some of them of the value of books. The letter that originally signaled my helplessness in the face of their indifference now helps remind me that such attitudes can be overcome. Many days some student of mine will come up and say, "Mr. Burke, I need a book," and the substantial classroom library I've gathered in the last five years opens itself to us until we find the right book, during which time we probably have had a conversation about other things, too. Such interactions have helped me to ultimately see books as conversations —with ourselves, with others, with the past, the present, and the future.

I mention this to assure those people who wrote to my classes that their letters made a difference. These letters have lived in my classroom, each letter kept in its own plastic sleeve, for these past six years; on free reading days, students often take down the binders (there were more than a thousand pages of letters all together) and read them, turning to other students to share something, or wrinkling their brow in confusion or disagreement. For the letters present to us not just erudite scholars, but soldiers and students, felons and lawyers, teenagers and eighty-year-olds, kindergartners and cattle ranchers.

I chose the letters in this book for the stories they told. This is not a book that sings the same song in so many different voices. I didn't want letters that preached how good reading was for you, that droned on about how it could make you smarter; I wanted the letters that talked about what a book means to a boy growing up in the midwest, to a man who'd returned from days in the jungle of Vietnam where he'd done things he'd rather not remember, to the girl who grew up in a family that did not understand her, to the man who has taken another's life and has learned through his conversations with books about the dignity of life and now ponders the very notion of justice that insured his incarceration in the first place. We have reprinted the letters verbatim.

Finding these people six years after they'd written was a search that reminded me that ours is, by its nature, a restless nation, one always on the move. Of the nearly fifty letters included here, roughly thirty-five of the correspondents had moved. The quest to find them helped me to identify another aspect of our American culture, which also helps explain why we love reading: Reading feeds our hunger to explore, to try on other places and different lives.

The title of this book derives from Walt Whitman's poem "I Hear America Singing," in which Whitman writes, "I hear America singing . . . each singing what belongs to him or her and to none else . . . singing with open mouths their strong melodious songs." Whitman honored all voices in America and challenged us to do the same; I tried to rise to that same challenge here, giving us a chance to hear the different praise-songs each writer offered on this one subject so essential to our success as individuals and as a nation.

It is in Whitman's America that I raise my own children, who just now are beginning to read and to whom I or, more often, my wife have read nearly every night since they were born. At night, as we settle down to read the next chapter of Roald Dahl's *Charlie and the Chocolate Factory* or Gary Soto's *Chato's Kitchen*, I like to imagine millions of people, of all ages, curling up with a good book; I like to imagine that I hear America reading the story we are always writing, which is our story, the one we never tire of hearing, the one I am very honored to share with you here, in this book, which because of its many voices, is our book.

Jim Burke
San Francisco

Dear Mr. Burke:

"How has reading changed my life?" My memory runs back to when I was seven years old. "Ding Dong!" My dad finally came home.

It was my birthday party. I was waiting for him the whole day. A week ago, he had told me that he would give me a big surprise on my birthday party. "What will it be? It must be that red skirt I saw in the shopping center!" I've looked forward this moment for a week that I was almost impatient.

I immediately ran over to him. He was very excited. There was a careful wrapped box in his hand. "Oh, my dear red skirt. I finally have you." My heart was pumping. Without my dad's consent, I took over the box.

"Oh, no!" My heart was sinking when I opened the box. It was not the pretty skirt I'd longed for so long. It was a BOOK! I was like falling down from the top of the world. "No, I never want the stupid book. Where is my dress?" I cried out. Tears were filled in my eyes. I've waited for a week for the useless book. I felt I've been cheated. How can he give me the cheap, nonsense book for my birthday gift? He didn't like me at all. I would never read it.

At night, I can't fall asleep. Looking at the big book, my anger was running inside me. It had ruined my party. Why did dad lie to me and said it was a surprise to me? Suddenly I grew curiously: "What is the book about? Is it so evil that I hate it and want to tear it apart?" I opened the book— *Chinese and Foreign Stories*—and read my first real story in my life.

There was a little virtuous duck. It's so ugly that nobody liked it. It didn't have any friends. Every animal around the lake laughed at her wherever she went: "Look at this little duck. Get away from her." Comparing to her, her sister was as pretty as a princess. Wherever she was, there were always friends around her. They would say: "Come here, dear. Come in my house." One day, they were playing around the lake. Suddenly, a little chick fell into the lake. He shouted "Beauty, save me." The pretty duck shook her head selfishly: "Why should I save you. I can't get anything." The ugly duck just passed by. It saw what happened and jumped in the water bravely without a word. It saved the chick. From then on, everyone liked to play with warm-hearted ugly duck. The story ends with a motto, which I remembered most—"It's the inside that counts the most."

I was ashamed when I finished reading it. I felt I was like one of the animals that only look at the outside of the things, but ignore what they really are. I liked the red skirt because it was pretty. But pretty outfit can't cover my inside. Only the knowledge can fill my mind. And reading is one way to get the knowledge.

I moved on to the next story. . . . I was deeply attracted. I can't put the book down anymore. I kept reading. I read during the break of the class. I read as soon I got home. Soon, I had a habit—I can't go to sleep unless I read some pages. Like what my mom said, "I fell in love with reading."

I fell deeply in love with the beautiful earth when I read "Our Home— Earth." I decided to preserve the earth like the guards who fight against bad people destroying the earth. I cried for Cinderella when she was tortured by her wry sisters. And I can't stop laughing at funny action of the little bear when it danced.

I read, and I learned. My mind was not empty with only pretty dress anymore. I was filled by books and knowledge. I began to understand what is true beauty, and to realize our burden as the residents on earth. I never felt I was alone and boring. I have books—my dearest friend with me.

As I grew up, my knowledge grew. I had regretted what I did wrong when I was young. But I never regretted to pick up the book on my birthday night. It's that moment I began to open the door lying between me and wonderful world, people and knowledge. It's reading that helps me find my true self and our value of living. I am still reading. When I get home after a day's tire work, my first hope is to lie down on the sofa, and read a book a while. It's the only time I can forget all the unhappiness. At that time, my book and I are the only two existing on earth. Every time when my dad asks me what I want most for my birthday present, I say it out without thinking: "I want books. I want to read."

Sincerely,

Grace Zheng

High school ESL student

⤳

*OPEN THE DOORS OF YOUR MIND WITH BOOKS, read
the red and white poster over the nun's desk in early September.
It soon was apparent to me that reading was the classroom's cen-*

tral activity. Each course had its own book. And the information gathered from a book was unquestioned. READ TO LEARN, the sign on the wall advised in December. I privately wondered: What was the connection between reading and learning? Did one learn something only by reading it? Was an idea only an idea if it could be written down? In June, CONSIDER BOOKS YOUR BEST FRIENDS. Friends? Reading was, at best, only a chore. I needed to look up whole paragraphs of words in a dictionary. Lines of type were dizzying, the eye having to move slowly across the page, then down, and across. . . . Shortly after, remedial reading classes were arranged for me with a very old nun.

. . . The nun would read from her favorite books, usually biographies of early American presidents. Playfully, she ran through complex sentences, calling the words alive with her voice, making it seem that the author somehow was speaking directly to me. I smiled just to listen to her. I sat there and sensed for the very first time some possibility of fellowship between a reader and a writer, a communication, never intimate like the one that I heard spoken words at home convey, but one nonetheless personal.

—Richard Rodriguez, *Hunger of Memory*

ᔐ

This little story is about reading. It is about literary classics, General Eisenhower, the Boy Scouts, patriotism and growing up in a small town in Iowa.

In the summer of 1945 when I was twelve years old, I read the classics: *The Last of the Mohicans, A Tale of Two Cities, Moby Dick, Treasure Island, Don Quixote, The Call of the Wild, Arabian Nights, Les Misérables, 20,000 Leagues Under the Sea, Silas Marner, The Three Musketeers, Ivanhoe, Uncle Tom's Cabin, The Count of Monte Cristo, Evangeline, Gulliver's Travels,* and *Westward Ho!* Precocious, you say. Another George Steiner or John Stuart Mill, you say. Or maybe you just go, "yeah, sure" with a sarcastic tone in your voice. Well, maybe I'm not up there with the great scholars, but I did do it. In fact I read *Moby Dick, Don Quixote,* and *The Count of Monte Cristo* at least four times and *Westward Ho!* more times than I can remember. And I have a medal from General Eisenhower to prove it.

Well, at least it's proof to me.

It is a small ribbon, one-and-a-half inches wide with three red and two white stripes of the kind worn on military uniforms. Hanging from the ribbon is a round medal about the size of a quarter with a picture of General Eisenhower and the writing around the edge says: "War Service Boy Scout Gen. Eisenhower Waste Paper Campaign." On the reverse it says: "Awarded for Extraordinary Patriotic Achievement in the Boy Scout Gen. Eisenhower Waste Paper Campaign—March–April 1945."

During this World War II campaign, the entire population of our Norman-Rockwell-small town—population 6,000—was exhorted to put out all their waste paper tied in a bundle on the curb. A city truck full of Boy Scouts would come around every Saturday and pick up the paper and pile it on the truck, haul it to the local junk yard where it would be weighed, bundled, stacked and sent off to the war effort. If we collected so many tons of paper each of us would get a medal from General Eisenhower.

How could I do all that reading and also work so hard for the war effort, you are asking yourself. It was because people were so patriotic that they threw out everything—*National Geographic, Life, Look, The National Rifleman*, sheet music, comic books—everything. If you want to know why an early Superman comic is so rare and sells for a lot of money today, it is because very few of them escaped the Boy Scout Gen. Eisenhower Waste Paper Drive.

We Boy Scouts of that time were rabid comic book readers. In one week we would collect a four-foot-high stack of comic books of every make and stripe there was: *Superman, Batman, The Green Lantern, Captain Marvel, True Comics ("Truth is more interesting and a thousand times stranger than fiction")*. From one Saturday to the next, we would split up the stacks and take them home to read, knowing that it was our patriotic duty to turn them in next Saturday. Many of my companions didn't really read. They looked at the pictures and jumped ahead to the next book, while I read every word, all the ads, and even took time to ponder how Billy Batson could turn into an adult super hero just by uttering "Shazam."

One Saturday while we were divvying up the stacks, I came upon a stack of strange comic books. The boys told me that they were called Classic Comics and nobody wanted them. Always attracted to the unusual, I took the whole pile. It was not long before I was enthralled. Here was real writing. Here were strange words. Here was a world I never dreamed existed. Of course, living in the Midwest, I was excited by anything to do with the sea, so I read *Moby Dick* first, then *Westward Ho!* and I have never been the same. I have never confessed this in public before, but Gen. Eisenhower is no longer around so I can say it. *I kept seven of my favorites.* I hope and pray that no soldier lost his life because I kept those seven comic books. I read them over and over and encountered words and names that were from so far away in time and place that I can still hear them ringing in my ears fifty-five years later.

Three years later, I was in high school. Our little school library was housed in one small room, but the schools in our town had been there since 1855 and I think some of the books had been there that long too. One day, having read all of Howard Pease's books about a boy who went to sea, I was looking around for something different to read, when lo and behold I came across some of my old friends. There, right on the shelf next to *The Prisoner of Zenda* by Anthony Hope, was *Les Misérables* by Victor Hugo. When I realized that the books were arranged by author's names, I found the others. They were all there! But, except for *Treasure Island,* they were without pictures.

Words, words, they were all there and they were my words. I had seen these words before; I knew what they represented from the drawings. I was familiar with a sword and buckler; I knew what a halberd looked like. When Don Quixote put a barber's basin on his head for a helmet, I knew what it looked like. To this day I could draw you a picture of it and venture to say that you have never seen one before. When Melville explained the difference between a right whale and a sperm whale I already knew what they looked like. There had been a two-page spread showing right whales and sperm whales.

There were others. I had long ago struggled with the pronunciations of *Uncas, Chingachgook, Queequeg, Quixote* and though I could not quite get my tongue around *D'artagnan, Bonacieux, Jean Valjean* (I would have thought he was a girl without the picture), it was an impetus that would later drive me to study French and struggle through *Les Misérables* in French.

Open Melville to almost any page and read for five or ten minutes and you will discover quickly the difference between illustrated summary and beauty. There is syntactic gold and metaphorical wonder in Chapter 29 of *Moby Dick*:

> The warmly cool, clear, ringing, perfumed, overflowing, redundant days were as crystal goblets of Persian sherbet heaped up—flaked up with rose-water snow. The starred and stately nights seemed haughty dames in jeweled velvets, nursing at home in lonely pride, the memory of their absent Earls, the golden helmeted suns!

From the Classic Comic, the scene where Ishmael and Queequeg have to share a bed, then board the Pequod the next day was beautifully illustrated and the pictures live in my mind. The scene in which Queequeg whizzes his great harpoon past the ears of Peleg and Bildad to come quivering to rest on a spot of tar that he has designated the whale's eye also lives in my mind. But the book, I say, the book, blast you (oh, excuse me, I get carried away by Melville), the book contains passages of thought like this one that I reveled in and applied against my recent Sunday church lessons. Ishmael is trying to explain to Queequeg the futility of religious observations because Queequeg has been fasting on Ramadan:

> . . . all these Lents, Ramadans, and prolonged ham-squattings in cold, cheerless rooms were stark nonsense; bad for the health, useless of the soul; opposed, in short, to the obvious laws of Hygiene and common sense. . . . hell is an idea first born on an undigested apple-dumpling; and since then perpetuated through the hereditary dyspepsias nurtured by Ramadans.

In the little town I lived in, by the age of 13 I had never even seen a real live black person. *Uncle Tom's Cabin* opened up that area for me. From the Bible, I knew what a Hebrew was, but I had no idea what a Jew was even though my best friend Dickie Bloom was one. *Ivanhoe* led me to investigate the matter further when I was astounded by the "Jewess" Rebecca.

Two or three thousand books later, after a lifetime of teaching English to adolescents, if I have any claim to fame, and if letters and notes from students and former students are any indication, it is that I have been able to entice them to read great literature through a passionate retelling of the stories and by helping them to mine the syntactic gold and struggle with life-altering ideas.

I thank Classic Comics (Classics Illustrated) for giving me a start; thank Gen. Eisenhower for my medal; some long-dead librarian for stocking the school library; the seven months of freezing cold, snowy Iowa weather that forces one to curl up inside by the fire to read; and all the great writers that opened up the world and the world of ideas for me.

Bill Clawson
English teacher

⌒

I also picked up [a] Superman comic book. Each panel, complete with picture, dialogue, and narrative, was a three-dimensional paragraph. In one panel, Superman breaks through a door. His suit is red, blue, and yellow. The brown door shatters into many pieces. I look at the narrative above the picture. I cannot read the words, but I assume it tells me that Superman is breaking down the door. Aloud, I pretend to read the words and say "Superman is breaking down the door." Words, dialogue, also float out of Superman's mouth. Because he is breaking down the door, I assume he says, "I am breaking down the door." Once again, I pretend to read the words and say aloud, "I am breaking down the door." In this way, I learned to read.

—Sherman Alexie, "Superman and Me,"
from *The Most Wonderful Books:
Writers on Discovering the Pleasures of Reading*

⌒

To Whom It May Concern—

That means whoever is awake if Mr. Burke is reading this to you. Don't let me keep you awake, go back to sleep, because this is a C.O.F. writing this letter. What's that? Oh, a C.O.F? That stands for Crusty Old Fellow.

Let's get down to why I decided to write this letter. I was born in 1931 so I qualify as a sixty-year-old. The rest of the qualification was, ". . . whose life was changed by the reading of a book." Sorry, but my life has not been changed by a single book, not even the Bible which has some damn fine stories. However, my life has been changed by hundreds, perhaps even a thousand books, because each book has a unique idea, one tantalizing line, one shocking proposal, one beautiful thought. Some books have even more than one great thought!

In the book by Tom Robbins, *Even Cowgirls Get the Blues*, he has one character say (This is a rough quote, so don't get picky, okay?), "There are lots of things to live for; some things to die for, but there is nothing to kill for." Isn't that great? Wouldn't it be terrific if everyone in the world could think like that?

Don't let Mr. Burke fool you: he can't make you read. Neither can I nor anyone else, if you don't want to, but if you don't read what has been written by people like Ray Bradbury (*Dandelion Wine*), John Steinbeck (*Of Mice and Men, Travels with Charley, Grapes of Wrath*), Richard Bach (*Jonathan Livingston Seagull*), Kahlil Gibran (*The Prophet*), Henry David Thoreau (*Walden*), Shel Silverstein (*The Light in the Attic* and *Where the Sidewalk Ends*), *The Collected Works of Robert Frost*, Jack London (*The Call of the Wild* and *The Sea Wolf*), the list goes on and on and you will not find those books that you really like. However, it is like I said, no one can make you read, all I can do is feel a deep, deep sorrow for you if you do not do this for yourself.

End of lecture.

Perry J. Rablin

P.S. Good luck to all of you, and you too, Mr. Burke.

⤚

> *The man who hasn't read good books has no advantage over the man who can't read them.*   —Mark Twain

⤚

Hey you big controller guy that tells us to do everything, yeah, I'm talking to you. So listen up, what do you think a world without books would be like? It would be a very boring and dull world. It would be like China (no offense China) where they hurt themselves in the past by burning their literature and other books. If we don't keep libraries in good shape you probably want to be like them either that or you must be a pathetic excuse for a human. We'll be hurting ourselves because some of the books will be soggy from the leaky roofs. Think about it and remember we will be hurting ourselves.

Jonathan

Fourth-grade student

⤚

> *By 2050—earlier probably—all real knowledge of Old-speak will have disappeared. The whole literature of the past will have been destroyed. Chaucer, Shakespeare, Milton, Byron—they'll exist only in Newsspeak versions, not merely changed into something different, but actually changed into something contradictory of what they used to be. Even the literature of the Party will change. Even the slogans will change. How could you have a slogan like "freedom is slavery" when the concept of freedom has*

been abolished? The whole climate of thought will be different.
In fact there will be no thought, as we understand it now. Orthodoxy means not thinking—not needing to think. Orthodoxy is
unconsciousness.*   —George Orwell, *1984*

⌢

Dear Mr. Burke:

Who am I? My name is Rose Hayden-Smith, and I am thirty-two years old.
I live in Ventura County, and am employed as youth development advisor
for the University of California Cooperative Extension. In clearer terms, I
am a UC faculty member who works in local communities developing
youth programs and serving as a resource for community organizations and
schools. I love this job, because it enables me to work with young people
on a local level, and actually see the positive changes they make in their lives
and communities. My husband is a partner in a large law firm, and special-
izes in transactional law, which is the kind of precise, quiet stuff you don't
see on *LA Law.*

My feelings about books and literacy are so strong, they have become a
defining part of who I am. I'm one of the lucky ones; I've always loved
books more than anything. Yes, anything. I have several brothers and sisters who are also avid readers. But I think that's mostly due to the fact that
in our chaotic household, the kid reading was less likely to be asked to do a
chore. (With six kids, there were lots of chores, too). Reading has always
been—and is still—a sacred activity in my family. Perfectly okay to spend
an entire day doing it.

As a child I read to escape. My home life was not wonderful. Like many
kids, my family dealt with divorce, drug and alcohol abuse, and occasional
violence. But when it got bad, I could always pull out *Little Women* and
live with a family that was loving, at least for awhile. It was a place where
fathers didn't yell and mothers didn't drink, and the idea of family was
sacred. Books kept me alive and gave me hope.

I lived on an Air Force base during the Vietnam War, and many of my
friends' fathers were pilots who were killed in action. I was seven, eight,
nine and I couldn't understand this war, and the way it was portrayed
on TV made no sense to me. My father flew and lived, their fathers flew
and died. . . . I was terrified. So I spent months reading about war, and
other people's experiences with war. Because the Vietnam War was too

immediate, I studied the Civil War. At age nine, I insisted that my parents buy me a subscription to the *Civil War Times* magazine. They did (to their credit, they always encouraged education and reading). Through reading, I was able to deal with my fears. My father made it through, and so did I.

I learned how to deal with emotions through reading. The town I spent most of my childhood in was small—2,500 people—and extremely impoverished. There was nothing to be proud of: it was an unattractive place, far removed from the mainstream (40 miles to the nearest doctor or movie), and full of people who had lost hope. But I could travel! I read and read and read and learned and learned and learned. When I finally made it to London (after college graduation), I knew my way around, because I'd been there in books so many times.

As an adult, reading has become no less important to me. My parents grew up in the South, and were young adults during the Civil Rights era. It was a painful period for them, and they were reluctant to share their experiences with me. So I found a book a few months ago called *Growing up Black in Mississippi* (by Ann Moody). It was a true account of a young woman's experiences. When I shared with my parents that I had read this book and my perception of what their experiences must have been, it was like a dam had broken. We have had several good discussions, and I understand their pain and experiences now, and have a better understanding of a critical time in our country's history.

Last year, I completed a masters degree in education at University of California at Santa Barbara. My emphasis was in reading, because I wanted to understand how people learn to read, and learn how to teach people this most important skill. I've also worked as a librarian (to earn money to put myself through college), a writer, and a public relations manager (to try to influence readers). Interesting careers all, and all related to reading.

I read a lot each day. For pleasure and/or information, a minimum of two or three hours each day, including two newspapers. I also usually have two to four books going at any one time. For work and/or information, another three or four hours a day. If I have to, I skip sleep rather than lose reading time. Reading replenishes me more, and I need it to live.

I read any number of books about any number of things. Fiction, nonfiction, poetry, you name it. I have a great collection of children's books. On my coffee table this week: *No Man Is an Island; Motoring with Mohammed; Fatal Vision; The Measure of Our Success;* Penn & Teller's *How to Play with Your Food; The Crown of Columbus; Milena;* and *The*

Complete Bookseller's Guide. (I had considered that as a next career, but I can't seem to bear to part with a book, so that's out.)

I'm addicted to reading. I can't sit still without reading. Even when I watch TV I'm reading. Even at breakfast, if there's no reading material available, I'll read the box. I am addicted, absolutely and totally. I suppose no addictive behavior is good, but given a choice of drugs, alcohol, or other negative things, I view this as a positive addiction.

My husband doesn't worry about me going to the mall; it is the bookstores he's concerned with. (He should be: I have several thousand volumes in my collection, representing a wide variety of genres and writers. I have also begun a collection of signed and rare books. Signed books include Richard Nixon, Richard Bach, Joseph Wambaugh, child's author Faith Ringgold, Ray Bradbury, etc.). We also take twelve magazines at home each month, ranging from *National Geographic* and *Surfing* to the *UC Berkeley Health Newsletter* and *Sunset*. My husband is an avid reader, too, and it hasn't hurt him, either. He's a handsome, football-playing, surfing rock-n-roller with an electric guitar who took me to see the Grateful Dead three times on our honeymoon. You can read and not be a geek. If you read a lot and well, and get a good education, you can make a great deal of money and more importantly, have a great deal of job satisfaction. We do.

I do a lot of volunteer work with literacy and ESL (English-as-a-Second-Language) students.

I have to be honest with you: I've never met an illiterate person who is an economic success. The correlation between illiteracy and poverty is very high. Stay illiterate, stay poor.

Money aside, illiteracy hurts us in other ways. The real power in this world and this society is knowledge, and until they can pump it into our veins, the only way to gain knowledge and make wise decisions (especially as consumers) is to read. People who don't read don't know. You don't know, you don't vote. If you don't vote, you don't have a voice. And it goes on and on and on.

Knowledge really is power; for many years, those who taught black slaves to read were severely punished; frequently, the slaves were put to death. There has always been a great fear on the part of autocrats that an informed populace presents a real danger, a perceptible threat to power. It does, and in a democracy like ours, it should.

The idea of public education in our society was based on the idea that people are responsible to their country. The responsibility of a citizen is to be well-informed, and an active participant in democracy. You can't fully participate in this democracy—or this economy—unless you read.

Why read? Reading is free (if you use your library), ecologically sound, good exercise (carry a stack of books to and from the library, or prop a book on an exercise cycle and pedal away), politically correct, and safe. You can travel anywhere with anyone in any time, at any time, just by opening the pages. It can also be a shared experience: read to each other, or try a book on tape. It's a good, inexpensive dating strategy we used.

If I could give you just one gift, leave just one legacy in this world, it would be to infuse in you an absolute passion for the written word. To have you pick up a book and let it take you someplace you've never been. To try to get you into the habit of reading something, even a few pages each day. It's a gift to yourself, and to your future.

My best wishes,

Rose Hayden-Smith
Youth development counselor

≋

    I live for books.   —Thomas Jefferson

≋

Dear Mr. Burke:

For me a book is a big part of my life. It makes me feel good and while I'm reading a book, I want to know more and more about it. If you really want to have a really cool adventure read a book. But you need to pay attention and imagine that you are the character of the book and that the things that are happening in the book are happening to you.

My life have change since I started to read different kinds of books. One of them was *When I Was Puerto Rican* because before I read that book, I felt that I was the only person who thought that almost everybody around me didn't like me cause my skin's color and because I am Latina. That book taught me that the people has to like you for what you are not for what you have, don't have or because what you look like. I'm very proud of reading books and very pleased with them. My life is not so hard like when I got to the USA. Now the books are my friends, company, and they make me feel better when I'm sad or when I'm alone. This is how I feel about a book.

Helen Garcia

High school ESL student

ᔆ

How astonishing the day individual letters lined up to become messages! Billboards unleashed their mysteries high above us. Signs on barbershops welcomed us to step inside. Lists at the laundromat instructed us about dyeing and lint. When I read the words "cream puff" for myself on the menu at the tea room where my grandma had taken me for a grown-up ladies lunch, tears rose in my eyes! The code was now mine!

—Naomi Shihab Nye, "Wealthy with Words,"
from *The Most Wonderful Books:*
Writers on Discovering the Pleasures of Reading

ᔆ

Jim Burke:

My mother died thirty years ago last April. It was 1947. I was thirteen. I was at a ranch boarding school in the California woods. Supposed to be very easygoing. My older sister was sort of grand and she went to the Bishops School in La Jolla, California. She died three years ago.

There was the rather mysterious teacher with cat's eyes and a great twist of auburn hair. She carried a Siamese cat into the living room in the evenings. We knew she had a past. After my mother died she avoided me.

There was the teacher with heavy, bored eyes; she read *Ramona* every afternoon after social studies. When my mother died, this teacher asked me to stay after class. She told me how to be brave and carry on the way my mother would have wanted. I asked if I couldn't check out a book from the shelf behind her desk. I wanted the poems of Edna St. Vincent Millay. She told me it was too old for me.

There was Miss Reitinger. I have an old notebook with a sketch on the cover. On the first page I have written "8th Grade Art, Miss Reitinger." Miss Reitinger has drawn an impression of me. There is a pair of harlequin glasses and a background of cactus plants and mountain peaks and some

Arizona artifacts I had brought with me when I came to the school. There is a beam of light passing through the background and into the foreground of the picture which explodes with stars and books bursting open and a few flowers and leaves falling from the books.

The day Miss Reitinger drew the picture we were sitting under a tree. The little worms were falling from the tree into her lap. She brushed them away without reacting to their squirming. I pulled her away from the tree and out into the sun near the river. She told me the headmistress had asked her to talk to me because I seemed depressed. Then she saw I was embarrassed so she told me how it was that she had come to teach at this isolated girls' school. It was a grim story but I thought it was sort of romantic. She had been persecuted by a man. After she told me all about that, I told her how my mother had begun drinking every day and how my father had sent me to this school to get me away from it all. While I was telling her all the things I felt, Miss Reitinger took my notebook and drew the pictures and there they are today and they are me as she saw me then. In one corner of the picture on the cover is a little star with tears falling from it. She never tried to tell me how I should feel. I wonder if she died too.

Jennifer Stone
Radio talk show host/writer

⁓

It's raining so hard one day, Miss O'Riordan the librarian says, "Don't go out in that or you'll ruin the books you're carrying. Sit down over there and behave yourself. You can read all about the saints while you're waiting."

There are four big books, Butler's Lives of the Saints. *I don't want to spend my life reading about saints but when I start I wish the rain would last forever. Whenever you see pictures of saints, men or women, they're always looking up to heaven where there are clouds filled with little fat angels carrying flowers or harps giving praise. Uncle Pa Keating says he can't think of a single saint in heaven he'd want to sit down and have a pint with. The saints in these books are different. There are stories about virgins, martyrs, virgin martyrs and they're worse than any horror film at the Lyric Cinema.*

I have to look in the dictionary to find out what a virgin is. I know the Mother of God is the Virgin Mary and they call her that because she didn't have a proper husband, only poor old St. Joseph. . . . The dictionary says, Virgin, woman (usually a young woman) who is and remains in a state of inviolate chastity.

Now I have to look up inviolate and chastity and all I can find here is that inviolate means not violated and chastity means chaste and that means pure from unlawful intercourse. Now I have to look up intercourse and that leads to intermittent, the copulatory organ of any male. . . .

All I want to know is where I came from but if you ask anyone they tell you ask someone else or send you from word to word.

—Frank McCourt, *Angela's Ashes*

⌒

Dear Fellow Readers:

What I like best about books is that they expand your imagination and show you life's possibilities in a way that nothing else can.

When I was twelve years old, I read Theodore Sturgeon's scary fiction book *More Than Human*. I liked the part of the psychiatrist so much that I decided to become one. I've been a psychiatrist for twenty years now, and I love it.

Sincerely,

Sandra Graber, M.D.

Psychiatrist

⌒

How many a man has dated a new era in his life from the reading of a book.   —Henry David Thoreau, *Walden*

⌒

To the Students of Jim Burke:

I was a "high school drop out." Really bad judgment call: I spent many years paying for that mistake, not only in lost income but in diminished feelings of self worth. But I was also a reader. I usually read about three books a week. Like anything else, reading is a skill that improves with practice. I guess you could call me a speed reader now.

At first, I just read wonderful, trashy novels. Then I branched out into nonfiction, forcing myself to read one book on any subject every week. By the time I made the decision to return to school, in my thirties, I was informed I had received the highest grade on record for the school's college entrance exams.

I am a criminal defense attorney now. I rarely have a client who has read anything other than an arrest warrant. Their lives are narrow and pathetic. The only information they have to base their life decisions on are the oral communications they receive from others much like themselves. Unfortunately, many other people I meet who are not involved in the criminal justice system are as narrow and limited. It is because they don't read. CNN is not the news. It is a production a television editor is staging because he/she has the film footage available. It is only a guide to some events that are happening on a certain day.

The biggest favor any of you will ever do for yourselves is to spend a minimum of 30 minutes a day with a decent newspaper. In a matter of weeks, you will be shocked at how uninformed most of your friends will seem. Maybe even some of your teachers! And you will feel yourself growing in ways you cannot imagine now. It will change your lives.

My favorite book? *John Brown's Body*. I carry it with me when I travel, and have read it so many times I have almost memorized it.

My phone is ringing off the hook, and I have clients in the waiting room, but if just one of you goes home tonight and reads something, anything, I will consider the time taken to write this letter well spent.

Good luck,

Sandra Medina

Lawyer

⋍

My best friend is a person who will give me a book I have not read.
                                        —Abraham Lincoln

⋍

Jim Burke:

I can certainly appreciate your desperate attempts to break through to your students. I can relate to your situation as well. Oh, if you only knew!

Not only am I a victim of my own ignorance for failing to fulfill my potential as a contributing citizen of the community at large, but I also find myself at a loss of how to inspire others around me to read books.

I am a prisoner of Pelican Bay State Prison. I am serving a life term for murder. I truly am the consequence of failing to search through books in high school until I could become inspired to a positive direction. Drugs and crime are what I resorted to twenty-seven years ago. Twenty-four of those years I have spent incarcerated. I am now in the sixteenth year of this life sentence. . . .

Books contain the solutions to the mysteries that are hiding inside each and every one of us. It's only a matter of discovering which book fits the individual's need. Unfortunately, that burden rests upon you as a teacher to match the children's needs with a book or books that hold the solution. I envy your courage and commitment to "finding a way" to pierce the void. I admire the ingenuity to reach out through the editorial page. . . .

I cannot point to any one book. Through my reading I have traveled the ancient trade routes on foot, or horse and camel's back. . . . I have sailed oceans, fought naval battles and survived capsizing in shark infested seas. . . . I have marched with the Macedonian troops of Alexander the Great and I've ridden in a tank with General George S. Patton and his 3rd Army. . . . I have seen, read and enjoyed the astronomical wonders of the past and present. What I see in the future is a society that cares not where we have been or where we might go—but a society blinded by pleasures of the self looking only for instant gratification. . . .

We learn from every book we take the time to read. Some have more information than others, some are more suited to our interests and needs—Ah, but some books inspire with a value far surpassing the worth of the biggest and brightest gem. . . . Look for it, ask for it, beg for it if you have to! In the long run, and ever increasingly the short run as well, events in our lives will mandate a need for information which is found nowhere else but in libraries.

Books. . . . I became fascinated with law books. Unfortunately, my introduction to those law books came about as the result of having broken the law, repeatedly. Had I discovered law books before breaking those laws, I would in all probability have become a successful lawyer. . . . I know for an absolute fact, based upon what I have read after it was too late, that I would have succeeded in some legal endeavor whatever it was. Hell, every time I read my monthly *National Geographic* I want to go to those wonderfully exotic far off places. With each issue of *Smithsonian* I want to visit the wondrous treasures that our museums hold. . . . From smashing the atom in a supercollider to the thoughtful prose of a Robert Frost, I will continue at forty-three to learn of facts and of mysteries through reading books. And I will honor my obligation to try and pass on to others what I have learned. My job is much harder than yours. I have to put pictures of naked women on the outside of my books and magazines in order to trick others into reading them.

More money is put into prison construction than into schools. That, in itself, is a nation bent on suicide. . . . We'll certainly need more prisons if our students won't read books. And if our legislators don't send our students books to read, they themselves should be imprisoned.

Hopefully your editorial will receive more illuminating response, and experiences of specific literature with which to inspire your students. Perhaps you can use mine to exemplify the consequence of failure and point out how easy it is to slide into sub-moronic idiocy.

Language is the crux of communication. We learn from the experience of others—that becomes written history, in books. . . .

Endeavor to persevere. I salute you.

Yours truly,

Eddie Burnett

I held my life in my mind, in my consciousness each day, feeling at times that I would stumble and drop it, spill it forever. My reading had created a vast sense of distance between me and the world in which I lived and tried to make a living, and that sense of distance was increasing each day. My days and nights were one long long, quiet, continuously contained dream of terror, tension, and anxiety. I wondered how long I could bear it.

—Richard Wright, from *Black Boy*

Dear Mr. Burke:

First, one of the most powerful arguments for literacy is contained in the *Narrative of the Life of Frederick Douglass* where Douglass writes about the power of literacy:

Very soon after I went to live with Mr. and Mrs. Aloud, she very kindly commenced to teach me the A,B,C. After I learned this, she assisted me in learning to spell words of three or four letters. Just at this point of my progress, Mr. Aloud found out what was going on, and at once forbade Mrs. Aloud to instruct me further, telling her, among other things, that it was unlawful, as well as unsafe, to teach a slave to read. To use his own words, further, he said, "If you give a nigger an inch, he will take an ell. A nigger should know nothing but to obey his master—to do as he is told to do. Learning would *spoil* the best nigger in the world. Now," he said, "if you teach that nigger (speaking of myself) how to read, there would be no keeping him. It would forever unfit him to be a slave. He would at once become unmanageable, and of no value to his master. As to himself, it could do him no good, but a great deal of harm. It would make him discontented and unhappy." These words sank deep into my heart, stirred up sentiments within that lay slumbering, and called into existence an entirely new train of thought. It was a new and special revelation, explaining dark and mysterious things, with which my youthful understanding had struggled, but struggled in vain. I now understand what had been to me a power to enslave the black man. It was a grand achievement and I prized it highly. From that moment, I understood the pathway from slavery to freedom. It was just what I wanted, and I got it at a time when I least expected it.

Secondly, a corney war story: July 31st, 1968 at Tung Hoa Air Base, Vietnam. There had been a firefight on the base perimeter the night before. I worked as a sentry dog handler. I hadn't been on that part of the perimeter where the fighting was, but I had been in Vietnam for nine-and-a-half months and I knew the war was wrong. With the corrupt regime in Saigon, there was no great issue of democracy at stake, no threat to American security, only an ugly civil war. It was painful to listen to guys laugh about the people they'd shot the night before, though it was a needed release. Uncomfortable, not ready to go to sleep, I walked to the small trailer that served as base library. What explains a dumb war? What explains basic human behavior? I remember picking out (of a *very* limited selection) *General Anthropology* by Jacob and Stearn. That's it. I just remember that book as a little bit of solace and understanding at a tough time. The story seems silly to me now. I might prefer a double margarita now, but it was nine o'clock in the morning then, so I went with the little book.

One more item—newspapers, nobody (none of my English teachers in high school) sang the praises of newspapers: you get to pick which paper, which articles you read and in which order. The TV news? Always it's the hard lead, a feature, weather and sports. Sometimes it's good to check the Giants first, then go to the funnies, then a feature, then a hard news item. Taken at my own pace. Bless the newspapers.

That's it. Give Frederick Douglass his due.

Sincerely,

George Cartter

State Park Interpretive Guide

⤳

> *For the first fifteen years of my life, I never read. I was just inter-*
> *ested in going out in the street and playing ball. It was only when*
> *I started going out with women who were more cultured and*
> *made greater demands on me that I started to feel I had to keep*
> *my end of the conversation up. . . .*
> —Woody Allen, *Newsweek* interview

⤳

To Mr. Burke:

I have read your paragraph. You say your student think books are boring. I think these just as individual student. It is because in my opinion books are the best way to spend time and improve our sence. It also our parent want us to do when we are teenagers.

In a long time age in China, there have a famous scholar. His mother don't want his son become corrupted. So she move one's abode three times. At first they lived next to a playground. Her son away play. So she move abode. They live next to the market. But he learn saying things like a market people. So his mother move abode again. In this time, she move next to the school. Therefore he became to read all the time. When he grown up, he is a very famous scholar in China.

In this story, we can know that in many years age, people have been know that learning is very important and read book are the major way to learn. So you student say book are stupid. Don't be angry. After few years they must know that books are the best friend in their life.

Jacky Wong

High school ESL student

⤳

You cannot open a book without learning something.
> —Chinese proverb

⌁

Dear Jim Burke:

Nearly fifty years ago on a troopship of Marines heading into the Pacific, I was given a book by "Pop," our twenty-nine-year-old squadron Communist (who cared, he was a good gunner). The book was John Dos Passos' trilogy, *U.S.A.*, and Pop lured me with the promise of "hot stuff" in it. It wasn't very hot even for those days, and by today's standards would be laughable, but Pop's trick worked: by the time I finished reading I was a raving radical.

That book changed my life. I'd grown up in Chicago: white, Protestant and lower middle-class, believing in a kind of Andy Hardy America, a high school jock wanting to coach if I survived the war. And now a book was telling me America wasn't all I thought it was. Lynchings, children working in mines, officials bribed, lands stolen, the heroes of industry ruthless exploiters of the weak, an endless list of things I knew nothing about. For the first time in my eighteen years I realized I was ignorant. Not stupid. Ignorant, because I just didn't know.

I was ashamed—and a little scared. I thought if I didn't learn how to find out what was going on around me, I'd end up as a punching bag for people who had learned. So until the end of the war I read every chance I got, everything I could get my hands on. Maybe I overdid it, because I came home wanting to write, ignorance and egotism combining to make me think people would be interested in what I said.

With a mediocre education and having lost three years, I had to play catch-up, and again was ashamed of my ignorance, at times publicly mispronouncing words and otherwise showing my inferiority. In any event, I bounced around schools on the G.I. Bill, every story rejected everywhere, and ended up with degrees in the writing program at Stanford.

I've published short stories and a novel, and for the last thirty-five years have been a television- and screenwriter. Let me express my admiration for what you're trying to do, and to that end allow me some thoughts, by no means to be taken for an essay on the subject.

Motion pictures and television are in creative bankruptcy because decisions are made by people born after 1950; in other words, those who've never known a world without TV.

Worse, TV and movies are explicit: the audience is passive, slumped there, just soaking up sights and words and sounds without having to think. Without having to imagine.

And that is what saddens me: the death of imagination. It has become so widespread it's hard to find any TV drama that isn't based on actual events—as if fiction has nothing to do with real life. I've written those "docudramas," but my current work, in feature films, is pure fiction, drama with a minimum of violence and sex, and with luck I'll keep doing it.

But reading is all imagination, and think about this: when I write a script I have only words, I don't have pictures to help a director and actors, I have to make them imagine what scenes look like. It's reading that makes the pictures.

There's a story among writers here. A father was puzzled by his kid's listening to old radio shows like *The Shadow* or *The Lone Ranger* broadcast on the LA CBS station. "Why do you like them instead of TV?" he asked. To which his son said, "Their pictures are better."

I wonder what would happen if your students turned down the brightness and contrast so the screen would be black. Or, easier, just shut their eyes. There would be sounds: voices, footsteps, laughter, speeding cars, no matter what, but they would be imagining, and just maybe the pictures would be better.

That's the beauty of reading: the writer is giving you a way of seeing his movie, and in doing so, you make your own.

My best wishes, and thanks for the opportunity.

Sincerely,

Stanford Whitmore

Screenwriter

⸙

I've heard a thousand times that ours is a visual age. But I cannot uproot my passion for words for fashion's sake, even if I wanted to. I suppose what I fear is that movies, however ambitious and excellent, can never do for me what a book can do. . . . Films, to grant them the tony name, are an art form, but in my heart a movie is still a movie, an entertainment, a voyage in the dark, a plush seat, a bag of popcorn. Technicolor, air-conditioning, the most luscious of escapes. I do not ask that it feed my soul, only my fancy.
    —Lynne Sharon Schwartz, *Ruined by Reading: A Life in Books*

⸙

Dear Mr. Burke:

Last year about the time I turned thirty-six and my age finally matched my waistline, bald, bearded, and long divorced, I resolved, at a time when I had come to feel guilty about my own performance as a parent, to find my father who had walked out of my life when I was an infant.

One of the few things I knew about him was that he had come originally from New England and so, when I left my job as a high school English teacher in Southern California to work in Washington, D.C. for a couple of years, I decided that I would probably never be in a better position to track the old boy down. In leaving California in favor of the Capital, I had, also, to leave my 15-year-old son Patrick, who lives with his mother. I missed him immediately. I missed watching him crack a double down the third base line, taking in the old Bogart flicks at the pleasantly shabby Balboa Theatre, and reading together from the cases of the delightful and astonishing Sherlock Holmes (when we bought Patrick his first pet, a hopeless, floppy-eared hound, he named it Watson). Perhaps it was the initial shock of that estrangement that finally got me thinking about parents in general. At any rate, one of the first things I did after getting settled in Washington was to arrange for Patrick to spend a good part of the summer with me. It was just after he arrived that I began my search.

Harry Arthur Gordon, Sr. was born on March 3, 1920, in Worcester, Massachusetts. He joined the Army during World War II and was temporarily stationed in Southern California, where he met my mother, Mary Ella Gray. They fell in love on the dance floor, moved, you might say, by the melodies of the old Glenn Miller orchestra. They were married a short time before he was shipped overseas. When I was born in 1945, my father was somewhere in Germany serving as a medic, and my mother thought it would be a nice gesture to give me my father's name. But when he returned, she tells me, he was not the same man. He hit the sauce pretty heavily and started hanging out in country-and-western bars back when that sort of thing was considered sleazy rather than stylish as it is today. When he left us a few months later, his disappearance could not have been more final had he been aboard Glenn Miller's plane when it vanished over the English Channel.

As it turned out, the very first step in my search produced the most important information. A friend recommended that I write the Social Security Administration to ask if they could help. I did just that and soon received a letter in return which contained the following intelligence: "Our records show that a Harry Arthur Gordon born in Worcester, Massachusetts on March 3, 1920, died on August 11, 1974." There was little doubt that it was he. I read the letter again and again. I suppose I was looking for something in it that wasn't there, some accidental bit of poetry, perhaps, that would help me feel the loss. But the letter was as dry and official as a past-due notice. I tried to remember what I had been doing on August 11, 1974, but could not. I showed the letter to Patrick. He made all the right noises, but I knew that the news had no more effect on him than it had on me. We had both just learned that my father, one of Patrick's grandfathers, was dead, and neither of us felt anything. I decided immediately to go on with the search. I guess I wanted to find my lost loss, and the only way to do that was to find out who and what my father had been. That, of course, meant locating relatives (assuming there were any) long unknown to me.

There was another piece of information in that Social Security Administration letter; my father's last known place of employment was Concord, New Hampshire. The long-distance information operator told me that the *Monitor* was the major newspaper in Concord. I called the city desk and asked if there was some way to check the obituaries for August 1974. No, I was told, they did not keep records that long. My next call was to the Library of Congress in Washington on the chance that they might keep copies of the *Monitor*. I discovered that not only did they have microfilm copies of the Concord paper for 1974 but also 1874.

The following Saturday morning, Patrick and I drove down to the library's Adams building and took the elevator up to the periodicals department on the fifth floor where we filled out the little request form and were, eventually, given a small box of microfilm. We inserted the film into one of the viewing machines and were soon flying with a considerable sense of anticipation through the winter and spring of 1974. We slowed our little time machine a bit as we approached midsummer and took a closer look at the paper. It was a typical, small-town rag full of local tidbits about roads and taxes and ads for furniture stores and beauty salons. We checked August 11th very carefully but found nothing. We were halfway through August 12th when Patrick grabbed my arm.

"Wait," he whispered. "Go back to that last page." I reversed the machine and eased back. Down in the left-hand corner, just above an ad for the Hong Kong Laundry, was a three-paragraph story with a headline that read, "Man Dies of Pneumonia." I glanced through the story quickly and there it was, my father's name in the second paragraph. And then I read the lead paragraph which I quote now in full:

A 54-year-old man who was arrested Saturday afternoon on charges of being drunk and disorderly died early yesterday morning in Concord jail.

I leaned back in my chair and took a deep breath. I guess I felt a little like Pip in Dickens' *Great Expectations* when he discovers that the convict Magwitch, and not the strange Miss Havisham, is his patron.

In the August 15th issue of the *Monitor* we found my father's obituary. It contained the names, but not the addresses, of his brother and three sisters, my uncle and aunts; however, the name that interested me most was mine.

"He leaves a son," the obit read, "Harry A. Gordon, Jr., of California." Apparently someone knew about me.

The newspaper had mentioned that my father had been pronounced dead at the Concord Hospital. The following Monday I wrote the hospital to request a copy of the death certificate which cost me three dollars and a two-week wait. From that document I learned that the "immediate cause" of death was lobar pneumonia and that "chronic alcoholism" was a contributing factor. I also learned the name and address of the mortuary which had handled my father's burial. I got the telephone number of Woodbury and Sons Funeral Home from New Hampshire information and gave them a call. Old Mr. Woodbury gave me the address of my father's sister, my Aunt Jean, who lives in Hillsboro, New Hampshire, not far from Concord. I sat down to write her a letter. Aunt Jean told me later that she'd been looking for that letter for years.

It was several months before I got around to driving up to New Hampshire to visit my newly discovered relatives. Patrick had long since returned to Southern California. My Aunt Jean and her husband, Hall Murphy, a carpenter, turned out to be wonderful people. They live among trees in the undulating New England hills. The Murphys made me feel perfectly at home and showed me around the little town of Hillsboro where my father had spent his youth and told as much as they could about him, which, as it turned out, was not much. On the first day there we drove out to my father's grave. He was buried near the bottom of a long slope in an old cemetery that Uncle Hall's late father used to tend. It was a warm, bright summer day. We got out of the car and walked over to the simple rectangular plaque. Hall had brought some garden shears. He started trimming around the marker as, I suppose, his father used to do. He brushed the dirt and clippings gently from the stone. It read,

HARRY ARTHUR GORDON
1920–1974
Private—U.S. Army

I felt as though I should say something profoundly ceremonial to mark the occasion, the end of the journey. But I could not. Instead, I said, "Well, Harry, you old bastard, you got away." Later, while Jean and Hall and I sat drinking gin around the kitchen table, I learned just how true that comment was.

I tried to get Jean and Hall to tell me about my father. Unfortunately, there wasn't much to tell and what there was to tell was embarrassing. He only came around every couple of years, Aunt Jean told me, and when he did he was drunk. He was the kind of guy you try to keep away from kids. He would get himself arrested every year just as winter was coming on and spend the cold months residing on the state farm. The rest of the year he spent working at odd jobs, sleeping on grates in Concord, and drinking. Mostly the latter, I gathered. Apparently, he was nothing more than one of the town rummies.

The next day I walked around the little town of Hillsboro. It is just a crossroads with a couple of stores and cafes. A small river runs along the edge of the town and the old textile mills run along the edge of the river. There was a little grocery store on the first floor of the building with a sign over the door that read "Gerini Enterprises." I walked up the old wooden steps and creaked through the screen door. I bought a cold drink and struck up a conversation with the old Italian at the cash register who turned out to be the enterprising Mr. Gerini himself. I wound up telling him why I had really come into his little store.

"Harry Gordon?" he repeated. "You're Harry Gordon's son?'

I nodded.

"Harry and I grew up together. Yeah, we used to fish and raise hell together. My family's owned this building for fifty years." At this point he launched into a lengthy history of the mercantile adventures of the Gerini family in Hillsboro. I don't know where I got the idea that New Englanders are tight-lipped. With a little nudging, I got him back on the subject of my father.

"Well, you know, I didn't see much of him after the war. He wasn't the same man. The juice, ya know. He used to come in here now and then and bum a beer off me."

Just before I left, I walked back to the cooler and got a six-pack of Bud and paid Gerini for it. I thought it was the least I could do for both of them.

I drank the beer back in the Murphys' kitchen with Uncle Hall and a colorful old character called "Stonkey" who was another boyhood friend of my father. He had brought over some old pictures taken when they were all teenagers. They were mainly hunting scenes, shots of grinning boys as proud as little Hemingways holding up a brace of birds or a line of fish. But Stonkey couldn't find my father in any of the pictures.

"I coulda swore he was in one of these," he said.

Hall and Stonkey got to talking about their fathers. Hall told the story about the time his dad, a deeply religious man, was struck by lightning while he was praying.

"He couldn't get his hands apart for two days," said Hall.

After Stonkey left, Hall and I had a couple more beers. We were quiet for awhile and then my uncle said, "You'll never get what you're looking for. You can't get it because you never had it."

"What do you mean?" I asked.

"I had it. Stonkey had it. Even Gerini. But you, you never had it so you can never have it. A father."

I told Hall about my stepfather, a fine and gentle man, whom my mother had married after I graduated from high school.

"No, no," he said. "You know what I mean."

I suppose I did. I had come to New Hampshire looking for something that didn't exist. There was nothing to find. It was too late. Hell, it was too late back in 1945. I had about as much to do with that man buried up on that long New England hill as I did with Wyatt Earp. He was just a name from the past.

I thought a lot about that the next day as I drove south through Massachusetts and into Connecticut on my way back to Washington. As I approached Hartford in the center of the state, I spotted a road sign indicating the direction of something called the "Mark Twain House," and it was only then that I remembered that Twain had lived there for many years.

I followed the signs to a gorgeous, completely restored Victorian mansion where Twain had lived while he wrote *Tom Sawyer* and *Huckleberry Finn*. Conducted by a theatrical student from Smith College, the tour was a delight filled with pithy Twain anecdotes. The guide told us how the family used to gather in the parlor every evening after dinner and listen to the author concoct a story extempore. He did so according to very strict rules laid down by his three young daughters. Twain was to begin every story with the knick-knack that hung just to the right of the huge mantelpiece. During the course of the story, he was required to work his way systematically from right to left through nine other objects laid out above the fireplace including a couple of strange figurines, a small picture of a cat, and a portrait of a soldier. The guide told us that the girls used to sneak into the parlor during the day and secretly rearrange the order of the objects to try to throw their father off, but he always managed somehow. I imagined the little girls squealing with delight as the old fox, puffing furiously on his cigar, feigned astonishment at finding the pictures of the cat and the soldier reversed.

And then I remembered the magical evenings that I had spent with Patrick reading *Tom Sawyer* and how he had roared with about an equal measure of amusement and fear at my drooling, snarling Injun Joe.

Maybe Uncle Hall was wrong, I thought. Perhaps I did have a father. Many of them. There was Twain and Hemingway, Crane and Hawthorne, Melville and Thoreau and all the others. Especially that American bunch. If I knew anything, if I felt anything, if I aspired to anything, it was a direct result of those long nights that I had spent marching their roads, sailing their seas, and dreaming their dreams. They had given me a way of looking at the world, a little something to pass on to my son. They had even given me a career. I knew that I would return to California, to my son and to my classroom where I would once again teach my American literature. And on my way a fantasy would play over and over again in my head. A fantasy inspired by a line from one of my favorite stories, "The Bear," by another one of my American fathers, William Faulkner.

In my little fantasy Patrick finishes reading *Huckleberry Finn.* He sets the book down and thinks for a few moments, and then it comes to him. He knows.

"Twain," he'll say. "Grandfather."

Harry Gordon, Jr.

⌇

He [the writer] must teach himself that the basest of all things is to be afraid; and, teaching himself that, forget it forever, leaving no room in his workshop for anything but the old verities and truths of the heart, the old universal truths lacking which any story is ephemeral and doomed—love and honor and pity and pride and compassion and sacrifice.

—William Faulkner, from Nobel Prize acceptance speech

⌇

A book means an action packed adventur of a who did it mystory a flying farry tail. But that's not all books mean to us they mean flying through the sky drifting through the clouds but still in your house with your head in your book your eyes skan the page as your imgenation tells the story. If you can read you feel these feelings but that's not all books are good for ther great for having an excuse for staying up late "Mom Dad you want me to be smart so let me stay up in till 10:00 all I'll do is read" books can come in handy they got me staying up till 10:00 las night "he he he he" I hope my Mom and Dad don't read this I think I stayed up a little bit too late last night I'm gettin sleepy knok out snor zzzzzzzzzzzzzzzz

Liz Johnson
Fourth-grade student

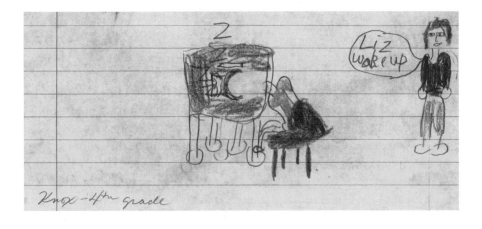

❧

This is what I like about traveling: the time on airplanes spent reading, solitary, happy. It turns out that when my younger self thought of taking wing, she wanted only to let her spirit soar. Books are the plane, and the train, and the road. They are the destination, and the journey. They are home.
—Anna Quindlen, *How Reading Changed My Life*

❧

Is reading important to you? Yes because if you don't read and if you can't read you can't learn and if you can't learn you can't servive and no one wants to die and that's why reading is important to me.

Stephen Schueler
Second-grade student

❧

Though not light, books possess an ounce-of-weight to minute-of-entertainment ratio that compares quite favorably to intoxicants. One school of thought holds that life in the tent so numbs the intellect that the only literature capable of sustaining interest is simple-minded, shallow stuff. . . . Others recommend bringing ponderous tomes that you've always thought you should read but never quite managed. . . .

—Jon Krakauer,
Eiger Dreams: Ventures Among Men and Mountains

∽

Dear Mr. Burke:

I am a retired teacher and counselor from the Los Angeles City Schools, now doing a volunteer teaching semester in Shanghai, China. I'm in a Foreign Language School, corresponding to our grades 7–12. The students must pass an exam to enter, and 90–95% of them board at the school, going home on Saturday afternoons for a day-and-a-half. They can study English, German, Japanese or French in addition to their regular studies in Chinese. The students I have in grades 8, 10, and 11 are quite fluent in English.

At the beginning of their English studies here they choose an English name and that is used in all of their English classes. Since some are already conversant in English, the names they choose reflect their reading in the past. I gave as a writing assignment "How I Chose My English Name," and a number of them chose from books. For example: Diana, from the goddess of hunting. Helen, because I read a book about Helen Keller and how wonderful she was. Jane, for Jane Eyre; John Lee, because it's like his Chinese name of Li Jung, but if he could choose another it would be Mark Twain; Blair, because she read a book about a Blair who was a clever and brave man. Jennifer, from *Love Story*; Harry, from *Look, Listen & Learn*, their English book.

Some just opened the dictionary and closed their eyes and pointed.

One wrote, "In grade five our teacher told us she would choose an English name for us & if we were well behaved in class we would be given the best English names she could think of. If we behaved badly, we wouldn't get a good name. I was very naughty that term, so there were no good names left. Mary, Diane, David, I was the only one called Ching Yuan, so I promised not to be naughty, so I got my English name Moses. From then on I have been a well behaved pupil & my friends all call me Moses."

George wrote that his name was too normal and he wanted to change it to PRATINITOOSE. So far I'm still calling him George.

I'm wondering if any of your students were named because of books their parents read.

(A side note: I'm in China because of reading an article about this program in the California Retired Teachers Association newsletter. My other volunteer work around the world has also been due to reading; i.e. Earthwatch projects in Poland, Vietnam, Hong Kong, Wales, Montserrat—the list goes on).

My best wishes to you and your students,

Helen Waterbury

Retired teacher

❧

> *The course will increase reading speed a little each day until the end of the term, by which time the student will be required to read* The Brothers Karamozov *in fifteen minutes. The method is to scan the page and eliminate everything except pronouns from one's field of vision. Soon the pronouns are eliminated. Gradually, the student is encouraged to nap.*
>
> —Woody Allen, "Spring Bulletin"

❧

Dear Mr. Burke:

What role have books and literature played in the life of the Sandstrom family (parents Don and Joanne, sons Donald and Erik)? Writings of John Muir and Colin Fletcher sent us into the Sierra for a 40-day, 240-mile back-packing trip (the John Muir Trail plus) when Donald and Erik were eight and six. *National Geographic*, Melville, Stevenson, Conrad, Bligh, and Cook infected us with an itch to sail the world. Since we couldn't afford to buy a boat, we had to read plans and construction manuals so we could build one. *Anduril*, the 40-foot trimaran we built (named after the sword of Aragon in Tolkien's *Lord of the Rings* trilogy, one of the "icons" of our family), has taken us on two circumnavigations.

The first trip, begun when Donald and Erik were thirteen and eleven, took us five years. Except for four months in Cyprus, the boys didn't attend school for five years—but we read about 800 books (from Darwin to Louis L'Amour). Donald had to take the GED in Rhodes, his SATs in Cyprus and Spain. He was accepted at UC Berkeley and graduated with a degree in civil engineering. Erik majored in English, graduated from California State University at Long Beach and now teaches English in Lodi.

When we returned from that first circumnavigation, Don couldn't find a job, so he went to the library and read books about building houses (different from building boats) and designed and built (with help from the rest of us) a home for us in Oakland.

Having read much about the Great Barrier Reef, Don, Erik, and I took a "quickie" 16-month circumnavigation to see it. That trip I at least kept track of what I read during the year (I had to fly back after twelve months to get back to work); the list is enclosed.

Reading, of course, inspired writing. I've written numerous articles about our travels for various sailing magazines. When book publishers wanted a book quite different from the one I wanted to write, we formed our own publishing firm, Earendil Press (name taken from Tolkien), and published *There and Back Again*, the story of our first circumnavigation (title is the subtitle of Tolkien's *The Hobbit*).

We wouldn't have done *any* of these things if we hadn't read books. We were inspired and empowered to do them *because* we read books. Other activities we can't/won't be able to do we *can* experience through reading books. Readers aren't limited to one life at one place and time in history. Past, present, future, and worlds that never were are open to readers. Through reading books, psychology majors (Don) and English majors (me) can learn to do things they never learned in school.

If you think your class(es) would be interested, we'd be happy to visit and talk about books/show slides of our trips that relate to books (Darwin's voyage to the Galapagos; Robinson Crusoe Island; the *Bounty* mutiny and Pitcairn Island, etc.).

Yours truly,

Joanne Sandstrom

Managing Editor, Institute of East Asian Studies

Say it, say it. The universe is made of stories, not of atoms.
—Muriel Rukeyser

ᕽ

Dear Mr. Burke,

My passion for reading began when I was young with the Hardy Boys mystery book series. I received a couple of the books for my birthday, and before I went to sleep that night I had read both books. The next day my mom took me to the library at my request to check out more Hardy Boys. When she finally found me I was sitting in an aisle with a bunch of Hardy Boys books in my lap. I had already knocked off one book just while sitting in the library. I couldn't wait to pick up another book and suck all the content from it. Thus, my reading career began.

Reading has become an integral part of my life. Many times I remember being tucked into bed by my parents, who thought I was about to go to sleep. Little did they know that I had sneaked a book under my pillow to read the moment they left. The next morning one of my parents would ask me, "Raziel, why did you go to sleep so late?" I would respond, "How did you know?" Well, I guess they had ways of finding out.

I think of reading not as something which I am forced to do, but rather something which I enjoy doing. Every morning for as many years as I can remember, I wake up, get dressed, walk to the front of the house, and open the front door. I bend down and pick up the *New York Times* and *The Wall Street Journal*. Reading these two quality newspapers for a half-hour each day has increased my knowledge of current events and enabled me to carry on intellectual conversations regarding them. I have also learned many new vocabulary words in the process.

Another influence on my reading career has been my dad's occupation. He is a rare-book dealer and so we have many interesting books in our house. I like looking at a first edition of *Huck Finn* or *The Federalist Papers*, as it gives me a sense of history and how old things are. In my house we have many bookshelves. Our living room has a whole wall of books, and in my bedroom I have three bookcases, including favorites such as *Forrest Gump, Into Thin Air, Visions, Don't Sweat the Small Stuff* and *The Haj*. Every night before I go to bed I meander over to my bookcases and select something to read, even if I have read it before. I have found that reading is the best way for me to fall asleep.

What I find the most intriguing about books is the amount of information a person can absorb. I think of it this way—with each book I read, I am taking someone else's knowledge and applying it to my own. Reading books, newspapers, or magazines will always be a part of my life, and it's hard for me to imagine a place such as the one created with the absence of books in the film *Fahrenheit 451.*

Sincerely,

Raziel Ungar

High school student

⁂

> *Just as, three centuries before, New England schoolchildren had learned the path to salvation along with their ABC's and had learned how to read at the same time they learned the tenets of their community, so farm children now learned from the [Sears, Roebuck catalogue]. In rural schoolhouses, children were drilled in reading and spelling from the catalogue. They practiced arithmetic by filling out orders and adding up items. They tried their hand at drawing by copying the catalogue models, and acquired geography by studying the postal-zone maps. In schoolrooms that had no other encyclopedia, a Ward's or Sears' catalogue handily served the purpose; it was illustrated, it told what something was made of and what it was good for, how long it would last, and even what it cost. Many a mother in a household with few children's books pacified her child with the pictures from the catalogue. When the new book arrived, the pictures were indelibly fixed in the memory of girls who cut them up for paper dolls.*
> —Daniel Boorstin, *The Americans: The Democratic Experience*

⁂

Dear Mr. Burke and Burlingame High Students:

Hi! When I was in high school, I hated to read. I really hated book reports because we never got to read a book that was interesting to us. It took me a lot longer to get through a book than most people and my comprehension was terrible.

Since reading was such a struggle for me, I decided the best gift I could give my daughter was loving to read. I read to her long before she could talk. Then, her kindergarten teacher had a field trip to the library. Andrea, my daughter, couldn't read enough. We went to the library weekly. I had to have something to do while she picked out her usual five books. So I started looking at books myself. I enjoyed romance, mysteries, and yes even history! (I detested history in school!)

I'm a flight attendant and have been flying for twenty years. I don't know what I would have done during the four-hour delays, or being snowed in somewhere, or even sunning on the beaches of Hawaii if I had not had books to let me escape what was going on around me!!!

Andrea and I went to visit my parents in Texas for a week. She didn't know anybody there and she read all 8 books that she brought from home. We ended up buying more books.

I think school is much easier for Andrea because she loves to read. However, I had to listen to her for a month on how much she hated *Julie and the Wolves* (a book report for 6th grade). She got though it anyway and even made an "A." Unfortunately, I had to read it so I could help with the report. She's right! (Not a fun book for me either.)

Because the city of Hayward is cutting costs, the library has cut down on its hours. I panicked when I read the library would be closed from December 20th to January 4th. We both checked out several books. One can only watch so many movies during Christmas vacation. The four-hour ride to Tahoe to ski sure went a lot faster with a good book.

If you do anything for yourselves, do yourselves a great favor and learn to love books. They made my life much easier and more entertaining. Books are a privilege!

Have a great school year!

Jan Delano

Flight attendant

〜

> When I was a child I loved to read. I loved Jane Eyre *especially and read it over and over. I didn't know anyone else who liked to read except my mother, and it got me in a lot of trouble because it made me into a thief and a liar. I stole books, and I stole money to buy them. . . . Books brought me the greatest satisfaction. Just to be alone, reading, under the house, with lizards and spiders running around. . . .*
> —Jamaica Kincaid, "Through West Indian Eyes"

〜

Dear Jim:

I've been going for fifteen years to schools around Los Angeles to talk about books. When the LA library burned down, I wrote "Wonderland" for a Women's Writer's West contest, and won first prize in the Fall/Winter edition of "Writing for Our Lives." Books were my treasure then and now.

Sincerely,

Yetta Speevack

MY WONDERLAND

That winter, coal was scarce
Our house icebox cold
My sister thought of the library.
It had a woodburning fireplace
Mama, stuffed in four sweaters, told us to go.

Child of struggling immigrants
No radio, no TV no time for telling stories
I stood wide-eyed with wonder
At the land of books, books

At a lady in a long skirt
With a smile she led me to a chair
Where my feet touched the floor
Brought me picture books of children
From China, from Africa from Europe and Alaska
A magic world of words and pictures

Different faces, different clothes, different houses
The children played games, laughed at jokes
Cried at hurts, got in trouble like me
I went often to the library even when our house was warm
The library lady brought more books
I never had enough of that magic place.

When I was in high school, Mama had time to sit and talk
"Tell me about the books you read"
So many favorites. Which to choose?

Mama and I never had a dog
But Buck's courage in Jack London's *Call of the Wild*
Made us shed tears at his endurance

One day I couldn't put down *Green Mansions*
I held the book in my left hand and did the dishes with my right
"In America a new style to wash dishes," Mama said
Startled, I dropped the book
"Oy Vey, from the library."
With reverence she dried the book.

On Saturday, Mama's rest day, she wore her navy-dress
Who could think of her scrubbing pots and floors
Sat near me eager to hear of library books
Harriet Beecher-Stowe's *Uncle Tom's Cabin*
Made Mama angry at such injustice.

I told the library lady how Mama loves books
She sent her Markandaya's *Nectar in a Sieve*
A Hindu mother's struggle for survival
Willa Cather's *My Antonia*, young immigrant woman's
Battle with the farm when her father died
Mama knew these women well.

Even the neighborhood hoodlums, the lamppost leaners
Who usually annoyed me on my way home
Who said, "Give us a kiss," while pulling at my skirt
Left me alone when I carried an armful of library books
Looked with respect at the books

"You should go to college," the library lady said
I wished that more than anything
"The library lady is right," Mama nodded her head
But where will we get the money? I asked
"We'll find a way." She did and I went
My Wonderland widened
In my next life I'll be a librarian.

—Yetta Speevack

*Have you got that article I wanted to read? I don't remember
what it was or what magazine it was in.*

*Do you have any books about people who get wiped out or
mangled?*

I need an ancient current event.

Do you have a razor blade and a bucket?

—Questions librarians have been asked, from Richard Lederer's
"Ya Got Any Good Books Here?"

⌒

Dear Mr. Burke:

One of the things that kept me occupied was that I teach Elder Hostel
classes, an antidote to teaching classes in San Francisco history at SF State
University which I used to do but can no longer. I stopped in the middle of
one of the hostel sessions to exclaim about what a joy it is to teach survivors
of the dying literate generation—those who used to and often still do read
books, who know about history and geography, who *get* allusions that edu-
cated people were once expected to know. At SF State, I felt as if I was
preaching to a field of stones, and when I realized that many of my students
did not know what the Civil War was or where Massachusetts is, then I had
to give up in despair. The joy of teaching, as in any worthwhile relationship,
is in communicating, and to do so, one must share a common language.

As a writer and historian, I've thought about this a great deal, because,
like most writers, I worry that I will soon have no audience to be writing
to. I hope that is not the case, but I'm afraid that it is.

I've found that all writers began as readers, voraciously sucking up
books from the moment they could understand letters, words, sentences. It
almost appears to be a genetic strain, because books do not, of course, affect
everyone that way. My parents divorced when I was four, and books
offered me solace and escape from a painful and insecure childhood. It's
probably not surprising that my first favorites were fantasies, such as all the
Oz books, but I moved on to history and literature, so that by the time I
saw Europe for the first time at 19, I felt that I knew London and other cities from Dickens and Woolf and Shakespeare and others that I had read.
From then on, books and experience reinforced one another, and have continued to do so, incalculably enriching my life and thought.

Unfortunately, the pace of life now is so fast that few people have the
time to read for pleasure unless it is such a high priority that they deliber-

ately organize their lives to accommodate that activity. I have done so, and though that has often meant material sacrifices (I have seldom worked 9–5), the return, I have learned, is well worth it. American culture, too, tends to be anti-intellectual, violent, sensational, and materialistic. Only when I was forty-one, and had the opportunity to live for a month in an old monastery in central Italy, did I realize that much of modern life, television, and pop culture in general, is designed to drive one nuts with frustrated desire masquerading as paradise. There is no peace in a shopping mall.

I have an apartment full of books and a good reading chair by a garden window. I am ten minutes' walk to one of the best libraries in the world. My friends read, and in talking, we unconsciously travel through time and enjoy the company of people we have never met, such as my mentor, Lewis Mumford, and all the historians, poets, and writers on whose shoulders I stand. I become more grateful as I grow older for all these men and women I have known but who never knew me, but who have helped me to become what I am. I hope that I can do the same for those who come after me. All those "helpers" are there for anyone who wants to go and find them. The libraries and the bookstores are full of them; we are fortunate to live in a country which once considered it a social obligation to provide access to so much knowledge. We are fortunate (for the moment) to be rid of those at the top who would have destroyed that heritage.

As one ages, one finds that the body will not do what it did when one was younger. A trained and curious mind, however, goes on, redeeming age, and making one ever richer in the process. The human mind is like an accordion file whose capacity for memory and for connection and synthesis seems nearly infinite. In this way, we work through knowledge hopefully toward wisdom, which is to be most fully human.

Thank you for writing your letter. I hope you got a good response. I suspect that you did, since those of us who still read are what Auden once called "ironic points of light," flashing our messages to others who still do too. And, by the way, my favorite poems are Auden's "September 1, 1939" and Yeats' two Byzantium poems. They make me marvel at what the English language can do when wielded by a master. My favorite novel is E.M. Forster's *Howard's End* which is a bonanza lode of wisdom.

Sincerely,

Gray Brechin

Historian

Dear Mr. Burke:

This is the information age and beyond even that it has become the electronic information age, with Internet searches, television, and new forms of multimedia springing up by the minute. However, when I became interested in designing Web sites and graphics for the Internet, my first inclination was to go back to books. I picked up a few books on the Internet and read about how other professionals created their Web sites and learned about the history behind the field of printing. What I read gave me the knowledge and inspiration I needed to work on a Web site of my own and create Web sites for other people.

The skills and abilities I learn from reading are tools I can use to put me in demand and open up new doors of opportunity for me. If ever I have a question or need help with an idea I am working on I know I can always turn to books; be it a reference manual, or a how-to book I usually find the answers I am looking for. When I read these books it's like the author is sharing their expertise with me personally, telling me their tricks and tips and arguing why their methods and ideas are good. Whether I agree or disagree with what they have to say, I've learned something, because now I'm equipped to form my own methods and opinions on the matter.

Even though how we read and what we read is always changing, the simple beauty of letters is always there. It's ironic that as we move into the future these ancient symbols appear on our most advanced technology. Books may be old, but the realm of ideas they can communicate is unimaginable. The media our society communicates with is—and always will be—changing, but one important thing remains and that is language, and therein lies the simple beauty and versatility of books. In an age when there are so many different types of media, you can always be sure that if you have an interest there is probably a book on it. It doesn't matter if you want to know more about baseball, molecular physics, or any other topic, books give you the ability to develop your knowledge at whatever pace you choose. Freedom lies in reading whatever you desire for whatever purpose.

Jacob Abrams

High school student

I can't look at the history of human communication without concluding—unfashionable as such a conclusion may currently be in the historical community—that a kind of progress has been made. Yes, we've lost some wisdom along the way, but I believe we've gained more. And I can't look at the magical devices we are coming up with for capturing, editing and making available moving images without concluding that they will help us make additional progress. I know this is hard to accept. Believe me, on an evening when each of my children lies prone before a different TV carrying a different vapid program, it is hard to write. The fall of the printed word—the loss of our beloved books—is a large loss. Nevertheless, the rise of the moving image, as we perfect new, nonvapid uses of video, should prove an even larger gain. All our enlightenments are not behind us. We are beginning again, and in this new beginning is the moving image.

—Mitchell Stephens,
the rise of the image the fall of the word

❧

To Burlingame High School Students:

I had trouble reading in the first grade, and for the two years after that my parents sent me to a private school. I wish I could remember what the book was that opened up the world of books to me but it seems to be beyond recall.

By the time I was twelve, however, I had explicitly defined why books were so important to me: in books I could find truth—maybe not the truth—but things very close to it. In the light of what I found in the written word I soon learned that I was being lied to: my parents were lying to me, my teachers at school were lying to me, my church was lying to me, and I began to see that society's purpose for me was to be just another commodity.

Two specific examples come to mind.

In 1964 my parents wouldn't allow me to go see the film *Tom Jones* or read the book it was based on by Henry Fielding. Imagine my surprise when I found the book in two volumes of my parents' "Harvard Classics." After secretly reading the book, I confronted my parents with the evidence and demanded to know why they hadn't wanted me to read the book or see the film. My mother finally eked out the pathetic answer that she didn't want me to hear the word, "bastard." I gave her the definition of that word and demanded they take me to see the movie (after all, it had won the Academy Award for Best Picture of the Year!). They acquiesced.

We had a set of the *Encyclopedia Britannica* and on occasion I would browse through it. One day I came across a word I'd never heard of before, *coitus*, and I realized I'd hit pay dirt.

Why read?

Because reading was, is and always will be: *subversive.*

Rick Bradford

Actor

Dear High School Student,

I like books because they are fun and you can learn new stuff. For example in the magic school bus lost in the solar system, I learned that the red spot on Jupiter is a big storm. Made of swilling gas and has lasted for hundred and hundreds of years. I also learned thay the biggest asteroid is 1/3 of the size of the moon. By Ryland Young

A novel is a question, not an answer.

—Richard Peck, novelist

❧

Dear Students:

I bet that so far all the letters you've gotten have been about reading. This one isn't . . . exactly.

When I was a kid (it doesn't seem so long ago . . . although it is over 4 decades!), I lived in a family that today's press would call dysfunctional. My mother was disabled and lived in a strange dream world that bore no resemblance to the real one. Since she was dependent on other people physically (she had polio when she was little and had a lot of trouble walking), she made up for it by being domineering. She ran everyone. You know how little kids need to learn to make their own decisions, think for themselves? Well, my mother didn't believe that. She told us all what to do, when to do it, how to do it, which hand to use. I was never allowed to make a decision of my own until I was practically an adult.

(Bear with me; there is a happy ending to this story!)

Everyone was afraid of my father, especially my friends. No one wanted to come to my house—which was fine with me, since I couldn't be myself there anyway, and didn't want my friends to see me as I was at home, completely dominated. My father never touched anyone, even us kids. Hugs were only on television. No one in my house ever said "I love you." There were lots of fights, yelling, arguments over stupid things that had no relation to what people were really angry about. Tension was the way of life. My mother took "nerve pills."

In a household like that I grew up alone and silent. I had no one to talk to. As a little kid, I just assumed that's how grown-ups are; I had no other point of reference. So I grew up quiet. Picture this smart little kid, surrounded by weird grown-ups, no sibling, no one to talk with, ever. I had feelings that no one else in my house seemed to have. (Now I realize that was because they were each a little crazy, out of touch with reality; I was, as silly as it sounds, the only sane one in the house, but grew up thinking everyone was like them. Now I know they're not.)

The only escape I had from my repressed, empty environment was books. I read all the time. I read everything I could get my hands on. Every week I walked a mile to the library and came home with a shopping bag full of books.

But books are only input; they're wonderful, but they're passive (although not as totally passive as television, which requires absolutely no mental activity). They're not something you do. . . .

So, inevitably, after escaping into the world of fiction for many years, I sort of drifted into writing my own. I began writing little poems, short stories. Nothing real deep, just fiction. Little stories about lost dogs, or science fiction. Nothing that came too close to my "inner self," since I hadn't been allowed to develop one yet. I was still completely dominated and isolated at this point.

But then I began writing to myself. A diary. A journal. Call it whatever you like, I began a marvelous, exciting, terrifying journey into myself that has lasted a lifetime.

Journal writing is like nothing else. It's like having your very own personal "shrink," someone to just listen nonjudgmentally to everything you have to say. In a journal you can say anything you want. You can be as stupid, as outrageous as you need to be. You can rant, you can rave, you can let it out. And I did! Not at first. At the beginning, it was just entries of things I'd done that day, what I ate, where I went. Dull stuff. But that was a necessary first step; I was warming up.

Eventually, my diary became my only friend. I had few friends. I was raised in such a strange environment that I never wanted to have anything to do with people. When I was a kid, I always wanted to be a veterinarian, so I wouldn't have to work with people, only animals. Animals after all, give you their unconditional love . . . not like people.

So I wrote. In my diary, I ranted about the injustices I perceived. At first, I wrote about the whole world. The universe. Nothing was too grand! Now I realize I was externalizing so I wouldn't have to focus on what was going on in my own family. Then I just figured I was being grown-up and worldly-wise.

I continued writing in my journal. For years, it was my only link to sanity. And as my family and my personal life crumbled and fell apart, the only thing that kept me on a somewhat even keel was writing in my journal. Why? I've often asked myself that. Why is it we can say on paper what we don't even dare admit we think? I don't know. There are many erudite-sounding psychological reasons, I'm sure. But I know it's true. It works.

As I grew older, my writing got more sophisticated. But still, it had grown into two separate styles. I wrote one way for school (college papers, etc.), and quite another way for myself. My own writing was, of course, far superior, but at that time, I couldn't admit that, not even to myself. That would have meant admitting that my family was crazy, that I'd grown up among people who shouldn't have had kids, and things like that were just too painful to admit.

Anyway I grew up, in spite of it all. And sanely, largely thanks to my writing. Eventually, I learned to join the two types of writing. I allowed my real self, my journal style, to penetrate my "public" writing—at least a little. But re-reading what I'd written was terribly painful. I shed more tears over my diary than I did over anything else in my life.

Try it. Do you have a problem? Something or someone make you angry? Write about it. Write what you think about it. Write how it makes you feel. Write how someone else makes you feel. But don't stop there. Don't just let it be a sounding-board for your gut reactions—although at the beginning, it will be just that. Take it a step further. Explore! Journal writing is exploring at its finest. It's psychotherapy, growing up and high adventure all rolled into one.

And it's not for "writers." It's for everyone. If you can think, you can write. Don't worry about grammar, spelling, all those things your English teachers seem to worry about. Just write what you think. If you keep it up long enough, your writing—and your thinking—will grow up. Don't let anyone tell you that you can't write; and don't let anyone read what you write—until you're *absolutely* ready.

Reading books is what got me started, but writing will continue until I die. I get raging furious whenever I hear some say, "I can't write! I got a 'C' in English," or something equally absurd. *Writing is nothing more than a visible form of thought.* Everyone thinks! You all have beautiful, wonderful, fascinating thoughts, the anger, the furor, the horror, the confusion. Sometimes those make the best writing. Writing is a passion, after all. If there's no passion in it—it's dry, book-reporting writing. You know what I mean.

Try it. You'll probably find you have a lot more to say (to write) than you thought. Something happens between the brain and the hand, connections are made between a raw thought and the written word that can be amazing! In thinking something through enough to get it on paper, you can often sort through confusions, straighten out what you thought was all messed up. There's logic involved in getting your thoughts on paper that somehow affects those thoughts. Helps make them more manageable. Lessens the impact, if you will.

I didn't know any of this, of course, when I was your age. I started writing out of desperation. I had no one to talk to, no one to help me. And it turned out to be the best therapist possible. A tailor-made shrink! Once I got past the hard parts, I was able to take control of my life and actually make something of it. And by that time, writing was such an integral part of it that it naturally became part of my professional life too. I eventually became a teacher (foreign languages), and now I'm a writer, too. I have four nonfiction books published, more than a hundred articles in newspapers and magazines, one published novel and two more to come. And I often think that none of it would have happened if I hadn't grown up surrounded by weird people who forced me to turn to writing when I was a kid.

I don't know if this is what Mr. Burke had in mind, but I hope you'll give journal writing a try. Where else could you find a best friend, personal shrink and lots of fun, always at your disposal whenever you need them??!

Best of luck!

Sincerely

Dierdre W. Honnold

Writer

Reading makes immigrants of us all. It takes us away from home, but, most important, it finds homes for us everywhere.
                              —Hazel Rochman, editor of *Booklist*

A poor white-trash girl, married at 18. Had four children. No college. Only education: books! Books that fell off the shelf at my feet, books that "called" to me one way or another. Millions of 'em. I'm not the Queen of the World, but I've come a lot further than anyone would have imagined!

Laurel Hall

Artist

THE FOLK TREE COLLECTION PRESENTS

LAUREL HALL

RECENT WORK

MARCH 6 ~ APRIL 18, 1993

RECEPTION FOR THE
ARTIST:
SATURDAY,
MARCH 6, 2~6 PM

⤳

Dear Mr. Burke:

I'm writing to you on one of my two letterheads—the one that shows just
how involved I am in the world of books. I collect them, create one-of-a-
kind bindings for them, and read them with relish (although they're best
with coffee, and I devour them like gingersnaps). I have bookcases in every
room, including the kitchen.

By trade, I am a freelance copywriter—that is, one who writes advertising, brochures, speeches, articles, satires and whatever else my clients need.
I've worked in advertising agencies on accounts like Levi Strauss, Sunkist,
Pacific Bell and many others, and for the past five years have had my own
business. (I'm also enclosing one of my business cards with my motto: *Service with a Simile.*)

This is a great career, and I came to it in a roundabout way, starting at about the age of twelve. I decided that what I really wanted to do was travel, meet famous people and have wonderful adventures. I knew there was little chance of a suburban twelve-year-old ever doing such things; so I wrote a story about it. Then I wrote another, and another. . . .

Eventually I ended up with a Master's Degree in English literature and a lifelong love of reading, writing, and the wonders of language in general. Along the way, I found out some interesting things:

- While practicing my writing, I also found that I was learning how to organize my thoughts, how to think creatively, and how to express myself effectively.

- I learned a lot about how to observe people and situations, and how to describe things, either objectively or in "targeted" ways to reach specific audiences.

- I learned that like any skill, writing takes practice—but once you have the basics down, you can have lots of fun.

I learned that writing well gives one a great deal of power. I've made people laugh, cry, get angry, and even go out and spend their money, just with words on paper. I've been able to give comfort and companionship to friends far away, and have given a piece of my mind to elected officials; I've spoken out about unfairness or unethical behavior in an office, and have praised the good work of others.

One of the best ways I've found to get people (of any age) interested in books and what goes in them is to help them make a book of their own—from scratch. It gives a unique sense of "ownership" and makes people want to fill the pages and tell some sort of story. Let me know if you'd like to know how; I'd be glad to send some instructions, or show your class in person.

Good luck and keep reading.

Margaret DeMouthe

Bookbinder/Copywriter

After paperbacks lost their allure, I converted to second-hand books partly because I couldn't afford new hardbacks and partly because I developed a taste for bindings assembled with thread rather than glue, type set in hot metal rather than by *computer, and frontispieces protected by little sheets of tissue paper. I also enjoyed the sensation of being a small link in a long chain of book owners.*

        —Anne Fadiman, from *Ex Libris: Confessions of a Common Reader*

⮑

Reading helps me lern and so lots of stuff. I like reading because when you keep growing and you keep on reading when you grow up you may be a famous reader and you may eaven sit on the stage and read so keep on reading reading is fun!

Samantha Law

Second-grade student

⮑

I learned from the age of two or three that any room in our house, at any time of day, was there to be read in, or to be read to. My mother read to me. She's read to me in the big bedroom in the mornings, when we were in her rocker together, which ticked in rhythm as we rocked, as though we had a cricket accompanying the story. She'd read to me in the dining room on winter afternoons in front of the coal fire, with our cuckoo clock ending the story with "Cuckoo," and at night when I'd got in my own bed. I must have given her no peace. Sometimes she read to me in the kitchen while we sat churning, and the churning sobbed along with any story. It was my ambition to have her read to me while I churned; once she granted my wish, but she read off my story before I brought her butter.

        —Eudora Welty, *One Writer's Beginnings*

⮑

Dear Mr. Burke:

In the Tucker household, reading is a god. It is desired and honored, respected and requested.

    I struggle out of the bottom bunk, to wade through the cramped room where my two sisters are still sound asleep. Ascend the cream carpeted

stairs, push through the heavy door. I tunnel through the warmth of the
bedspread, resting in the crease between mum and dad. Dad on the right,
mum on the left, always. After silent but firm prods to the back, my father
stumbles from bed into his tired green bathrobe and answers the demand
for tea and "tote." He returns with two cups of tea, a mug of sugared warm
milk, toast slathered in butter and jam, all balanced precariously atop a pile
of well-worn books. At 5 a.m., the routine of childhood has begun.

Seventeen years of experience, and I still remember fondly those early
mornings hiding from the alligators of the world in books. My mother's
veins showing lavender underneath her skin, and my father turning pages
with unparalleled enthusiasm. We visited the busy world of Richard Scarry,
and washed pinafores in the creek with Mrs. Hedgehog. We destroyed the
nerves of the Park Plaza staff with *Eloise* and decoded the riddles of Dr.
Seuss. This is the stuff that a love of language is made of.

Lucrative "chapter books" came next. The seemingly desperate importance of the every day in elementary school was concluded as childhood
had begun: beneath a down comforter. The three Tucker sisters would flop
on top of mum's short legs and listen to the adventures of Laura Ingalls
Wilder whispering across the prairie. It was a time of good living, nutritious
growth, and cultivation of the mind.

Then, lumbering down the road, came the trials of high school. The
stomping ground of rote memorization. Original thought, while in existence, was rare. The intimacy of reading all but vanished as it was lost under
the stench of rotting trigonometry problems. I followed my peers during
the school week, dodging the terrors of sitting quietly in the pursuit of
more sleep or fast nights.

True reading became a sporadic event. Somewhat by the force of
ingrained nature, I would stumble upon a quiet afternoon. In the backyard,
without friends or clatter, kept awake by the itchy, wild grass. I could read.
Bugs skipping across the pages and the sunlight warming the part in my
hair. I could then return momentarily to the scent of sugared milk and the
color of the filtered sunlight of five in the morning.

When the absurd drama cleared, at the start of my senior year, I finally rec-
ognized my thirst for the days of reading past. I withdrew into a world which
had become relatively foreign to me. A former English teacher gave me the
opportunity to do just that for my last year in high school. To think, to read,
to grow, in a self-designed Humanities class of my own creation. Filled with
the clarity brought by a lazy summer, I was left quietly in an English classroom filled with all sorts of books. I selected books by running an index fin-

ger over hundreds of spines and blindly choosing the one that felt right. I could then retreat into a sunken couch tucked away in the classroom corner and read until the violence of the school bell sent me packing back into the real world. It was the perfect experience to revitalize my mind.

I am convinced that it was early mornings that propelled me through elementary school and rescued me from the doldrums of secondary education. It's a strain to imagine who I would be today without those sacred early morning hours, except to observe my peers who loathed literature, abandoned *The Scarlet Letter* and dismissed Hemingway as irrelevant. It is from this pack of American reading norms that I now cower.

And so this fairy tale of reading has a happy ending. I have regained my footing on familiar and preferred ground. Year after year, my head was in the hands of my teachers, but my heart was searching all along for a mug of sugared warm milk and a good story.

Megan Tucker
High school student

⌒

"What is the use of a book," thought Alice, "without pictures or conversations?"
—Lewis Carroll, *Alice's Adventures in Wonderland*

⌒

Dear Mr. Burke:

I have a confession to make to your students. When I was growing up, my parents strongly encouraged me to read, and I grew up secretly enjoying books although I pretended with many of my friends not to like reading for all of the usual reasons, particularly, because it didn't seem to be the male, athletic or sociable thing to be doing. Now that I have achieved some success, I can tell you that reading has been and continues to be one of the most important and enjoyable uses I make of my time, and that I truly owe any success to the books I've read.

As a lawyer I needed to persuade judges and juries to accept the position for which I was arguing. As a judge, my most important function is to communicate what is significant about the evidence I hear so that a reader can understand why I've reached a particular decision. Reading empowered me by giving me the language and vocabulary to express my observations, thoughts, and ideas. As a judge, I constantly listen to and read arguments from attorneys, picking and choosing the argument that is more persuasive, better expressed, and better supported. Conversely, I see people all the time who are misunderstood, taken advantage of, or even unable to get a job, because they can't express what they want to say. We live in a busy world where people won't take the time to find out what you really mean to say if you can't express yourself clearly and quickly.

Reading continues to present me with more ideas than I could ever achieve on my own or even by talking to everyone I personally know. I value what I learned about life and human experiences from Shakespeare, Thomas Wolfe or Ernest Hemingway as much or more than my law books. I read books as well as other judges' decisions to get ideas as to how to handle situations similar to those with which I am concerned. The ideas and concepts I read about enable me to choose wisely how to respond to a particular problem or situation, whether it's what to do about a particular case, who to pick for President of the United States, which television to buy, or how to fix the leaky faucet in my house. When I was younger, I thought no one took advantage of those who were strong and tough. Now that I'm older, I've learned there's a lot of ways to part a tough fool from his money, but people who are well read tend not to be fools.

Of course, reading provides me with pleasures, explorations, emotions, and adventures that I could and would never experience on my own. But I really believe that reading is like playing basketball or piano—you have to work at it and practice for a while before you enjoy it. No movie or television show could ever be as powerful as my own imagination stimulated by what I read because no other medium is so unlimited by time, space, or budgetary constraints. Television to me is a spectator sport, whereas reading is truly interactive.

When people are in school, too many people are too polite to tell them that the opposite of being well read is being ignorant. Being ignorant as an adult results in a lot of penalties and disadvantages. I'm convinced that reading opened doors to my future; if I had not practiced my reading, I would have slammed the doors shut.

Sincerely,

Alan K. Goldhammer

Judge

*We have talked long enough in this country about equal rights.
We have talked for a hundred years or more. It is time now to
write the next chapter—and to write it the books of law.*
— Lyndon Baines Johnson,
from his first address to Congress as President,
November 27, 1963

∽

RIGHT NOW I CHOOSE SADNESS

*She wrote me today and asked: Is everyone there on Death Row? At first,
I said no and then I begun to wonder, could it be so.* (Inspired by the kids at
Point Arena Elementary School who sent me their poems and letters.)

It was a glorious day, one where the sun kisses you the moment your
eyes are open, and you know something wonderful is going to happen,
although you have no idea what it is. I was feeling like a young eagle aware
for the first time of what his wings were for—dancing in and out of clouds.

People began early that morning calling me a poet, and I didn't know
what they meant by (A POET), nor did I consider myself one. I was merely
writing words. You see my English, my command of grammar and pen-
manship has always been awfully bad (awfully bad).

One day I will write my life story, not all of it, just the highlights and
low lights. Life seems to dangle between the two lights. But this is not the
time for my life story, just a short story, one piece of the pie.

If I had any lettermanship of communicating with the world beyond
these walls, my lettermanship had to improve. I have written thousands of
letters. Most people write tens of letters in a lifetime, but I've written thousands already. The letters became another arm, an extension of myself
reaching above, through, and beyond these walls, caressing people the way
I wanted them to be caressed. Touching them where they feel. Letter writing for me became an art, something I wasn't aware of at the time. Only
when I got into writing poetry, my life, my life was the melody. I discovered my essence was a poem. But I still did not consider myself a poet.

My first poems weren't real and I felt that void deep inside the heart that
does not beat nor pump blood. I knew I was consciously trying to attain
and be something I am not—trying to be the moon blowing when I was the
sun shining. I let myself be and my pen woke up like a tempest wakes up a
drought-stricken land. My first true poem flowed in one stroke, "No
Beauty in Cell Bars." It shocked my mentor, and upon reading it, all she
could say with eyes full of tears was "OUTRAGEOUS," that I must have

been listening in class, although I lingered outside the room, always wanting to avoid crowds and closed-in spaces. From that day on my mentor and others considered me a poet. Yet I didn't. I thought of myself as too uneducated with the nuances of English and its grammar to be a writer, a poet. However, since that day my writing went into automatic and I knew from then on I could write for exercise, to relieve tension. I would write for the pleasure it gave me to reread something written by my pen, but at times, it would seem alien to me. I would often wonder where it came from.

People from all walks of life would compliment me on my writing. They would say things like "I never liked poetry, but I like yours." I would say to myself, "They are just being polite, kind to a fellow human being." But their words lingered with me and evoked even more words, thoughts, letters and poems inspired by life and the people around me. I'd find myself naturally tailor-making them, innately tapping a pool of realness and truth in combination I never knew existed inside. I'd share the realness with people just to see the magic of their smile, if only expressed in their letters by way of a smiling face. It sent floods of joy to my soul like music. But I still didn't think of myself as a poet.

But this day—where every flower seemed to be blooming on every hillside in lucrative colors, where every baby bird seemed to have its fill of seed, and was basking in the sweet sunshine—I knew this day would be different. So, as I had done each morning since my introduction to poetry, I went to meet my mentor. I usually wore dark shades to hide my eyes, but when my mentor unleashed the marvelous surprise, the glasses no longer served their purpose. She said "Spoon, guess what?" Then she went on to say, "I read your poetry at this school," and reached into a desk and pulled out a bundle of letters and tossed them to me, "and the kids loved your poetry and wrote these poems and letters to you."

I hardly ever smiled or took off my shades even on the most wonderful of days. I'd keep the wonder of it all inside of me. But, as I began to read the poems and letters, I was unable to contain the magnificence, the joy jumping off the pages into my heart and soul. The shades could not hide the happiness, so I took them off. For the first time I ran around showing the poems and letters I had received from the kids, sharing my poetry with people, people I didn't like or know. My existence on this malted rock finally had meaning—a beat, a pulse. The whole day was enhanced with such joy, I walked around smiling inside out. I truly felt like a poet.

I had hoped to write them all back to share my thoughts with them and to thank them all. Their poems and letters were real and full of life and greeted me with tremendous beauty, the beauty of a butterfly in the warmth of the sun. I felt like the sky in all its glory. I said to myself "THANK YOU" for taking me beyond the walls of San Quentin. . . .

The very next day I was summoned to an office, and as soon as the door opened a frost feeling hit me. Something (deep inside) told me that the powers that be could not have someone smiling inside and outside, from behind bars—where the only right one has is to breathe, and they made it plain that if you become too real even that one right is prohibited. Finally, they spoke, "Sorry, you cannot keep any of the poems and letters." And the kids' letters and poems were taken from my hands. I sat there in silence for a few moments, as people filed by. I put my shades and frown back on, and without a word I got up and left, forgetting the misery of where I was. I was seeking a place to be alone. I realized in Hell it is always hot, there is no shade.

People found out what had happened, and as they passed me by they would say, "At least you got to see them." The poems and letters—at least you got to see them, people say. Words sometimes do not fill the spaces, just like one drop of water does not make an ocean or a river.

As I sat in a dark cage, I heard sad music, and silence to assuage the deep wound in my heart and spirit. I thought of their poems and letters, of how naturally they went to my heart—no detours. Still, their letters and poems lie solid within my heart and spirit. Now I choose sadness over happiness, for I feel like a river that has been drained.

Spoon Jackson

⌣

So I went off to another town to find work. It was the same as at home so far as dreariness and lack of hope and blunted impulses were concerned. But one thing did happen that lifted me up. In a pile of rubbish I found a copy of Milton's complete works. The back was gone and the book was yellowed. But it was all there. So I read Paradise Lost *and luxuriated in Milton's syllables and rhythms without ever having heard that Milton was one of the greatest poets of the world. I read it because I liked it.*

—Zora Neale Hurston, *Dust Tracks on the Road*

⌣

Dear High School Student,

I have a Rocking Book, Godzilla is the title. I can't wait for you to read it. It is about Godzilla trying to destroy the city. You will think it is cool. You can read it if you want!

Your friend,

Mickey Hemenway

Third-grade student

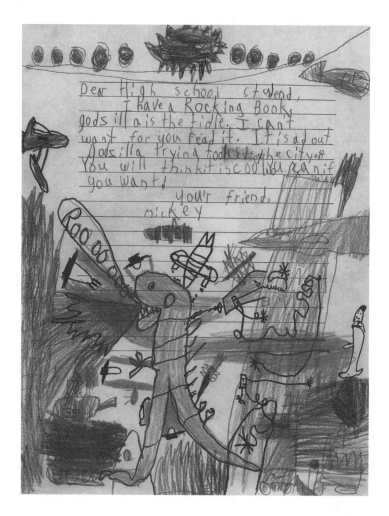

Dear Mr. Burke,

Your letter in *The Chronicle* moved me. I retired from teaching after 22 years in an inner-city Oakland high school. That was 1981 and it's clear to me that conditions have deteriorated frighteningly in the last decade.

I have one story that might be of some use to you. I had a class of bright eleventh graders—an English class. They were not College Prep students, but they were lively, pleasant, and hard-working. One of the books we read was *Choice of Weapons* by Gordon Parks. You may be familiar with him. He was the first black *Life* magazine photographer. One young lady, a cheerleader and "big girl on campus," told me she had never before read a book to the end but that one showed her something she didn't know she could find in books—people like herself and people she might never know. It started her on her way around the library. She read constantly. In twelfth grade she applied for and was awarded a four-year scholarship to Scripps College where she did very well indeed.

I'm sure you're doing noble work. I was really pleased to know someone cares enough to do something.

Sincerely,

Frances Whitney

Retired teacher

⌒

*There were few books in our house: a couple of thin stories read to me as a child in Pennsylvania (*The Little Boy Who Ran Away, *an* Uncle Remus *sampler), the* M *volume of the* World Book Encyclopedia *(which I found one day in the trash behind the secondhand store), and the Hollywood tabloids my mother would bring home from work. I started buying lots of Superman and Batman comic books because I loved the heroes' virtuous omnipotence—comic books, our teachers said, were bad for us—and, once I discovered them, I began checking out science fiction novels from my grammar school library. Other reading material appeared—the instructions to my chemistry set, which I half understood and only half followed, and, eventually, my astronomy books, which seemed to me to be magical rather than discursive texts. So it was that my early intrigue with literacy—my lifts*

*and escapes with language and rhythm—came from comic books
and science fiction, from the personal, nonscientific worlds I created with bits and pieces of laboratory and telescopic technology,
came, as well, from the Italian stories I heard my uncles and parents tell.*

—Mike Rose,
*Lives on the Boundary: The Struggles and
Achievements of America's Underprepared*

A few thoughts on books for your students,

I'm currently the Managing Editor of Special Reports for *Variety*, and a
professional journalist/screenwriter, so it might seem like I would naturally
have been a great student of English and/or literature. But my high school
years were in the 60's, and I was drawn to rock-and-roll and rebellion and I
flunked English.

So I feel qualified to speak about books not as a professional, but someone who just loves the rush of life, art, music, love, etc.

I remember ditching school and sitting in a grove of trees reading T.S.
Eliot's "Prufrock" and "Waste Land."

Running away from home, inspired by the poetry of Ginsberg and
Dylan and Guthrie (Woody). Before that, in junior high, discovering,
thanks to my 8th grade teacher, the difference between James Bond novels
and Camus' *The Plague*. And having my life changed by Steinbeck's stories
of regular people.

Kerouac fueled my dreams, Burroughs blew my mind, and later in life,
Rilke opened up doors to the essence of life itself.

I just went to Paris, and took Michael Leiris' *Manhood* with me, and
Kerouac's *Satori in Paris*.

B. Traven's *Treasure of the Sierra Madre* and *The Night Visitor* are para-
bles that will teach you all you ever need to know about *greed* and *love*.

Simone de Beauvoir's *All Men Are Mortal* is a great vampire-type tale
that I have been trying for 16 years to make into a film. It's the best Euro-
pean history ever written for the lovers of fantasy-fiction.

When I was in second grade, Richard Halliburton's *Complete Book of
Marvels* taught me that the world was a place of wonder, dreams, passion,
beauty, history, danger, mystery. . . . I'm just a forty-one-year-old ex-hippie
rock-n-roller movie buff who couldn't live without *BOOKS*!

Seize the day!! Read! LIVE!!!

Regards,

Steven Gaydos

Managing Editor, Special Projects, *Variety*

P.S. See *The Wild Bunch* when it is reissued and discuss its profound politics as opposed to today's *idiotic* violent films. It is a *great* piece of *film literature.*

⤳

Read the greatest stuff but read the stuff that isn't so great, too. Great stuff is very discouraging. If you read only Beckett and Chekhov, you'll go away and only deliver telegrams at Western Union. —Edward Albee, Playwright

⤳

To the students of Jim Burke:

There is an old country/western song that goes, "Let's get drunk and be somebody." What the song writer is saying, of course, is that while you're drunk you can easily convince yourself that you are somebody, despite all the evidence to the contrary. While drunk you are witty, amusing, sexy, bright, good looking, intelligent, self-confident, and full of self-esteem. On the morning of the hangover you discover that you were really dull, ignorant, gross, ugly, stupid, and full of nothing but sour beer and b.s.

Reading books is a way to get to be somebody without the hangover. Book learning, as it used to be called, is the one sure route to success, outside of hard rock and football. If you can't be another Madonna or Joe Montana, you had better learn to read books. And even superstars have to know what they are talking about. Otherwise, they may make fools of themselves, the way vice presidents sometimes do.

TV and movies are fun. They entertain you. But the only things they exercise are your ears and eye balls. Your brain just lies there, collecting fat. Reading books is aerobics for the brain. Reading engages you in a relationship with the author, *mano a mano*, that will burn off the fat and leave you feeling witty, amusing, sexy, bright, good looking, intelligent, self-confident and full of self-esteem. And no morning after. So, read.

Sincerely,

Donald Daniels

Retired

⟨⟩

Some of my best friends can be found only between the covers of certain books.   —attributed to Walt Whitman

⟨⟩

Dear Mr. Burke,

When I think about what reading means to me, two important places come to mind: the small neighborhood library down the street from my house, and my cozy little pink bedroom, which has looked the same for more than eight years. These two places have provided the atmosphere in which I can think and feel, and discover so much about the world.

Some of my first memories are of my parents propping me up on my bed next to them and reading me amazing stories about everything from magic fairies to field mice falling asleep in their soup. Soon my favorite bedtime plea became, "Just one more," or "Read it again!" And eventually I was old enough for Pajama Story Time at the neighborhood library down the street.

A little after dinner time, my sister and I would march down the street in our pajamas, sometimes holding our favorite stuffed animal, for a story in the Lions Den (the children's room of the library). I vaguely remember my first trip to this special gathering. I was so excited after all those years of seeing my sister indulge in this summer-evening event without me, I couldn't believe it was finally my turn, too. It was all that I had hoped for and more. The stories were fantastic. Soon enough I began to take my own after-school trips to the Lions Den to check out my three books for the week.

When we finally returned from the library (it usually took at least a half-hour to narrow down my choices), I would rush up to my room to set them out in the order they would be read each night. Looking back, I am amazed at how much even these children's books made me feel.

I was so happy for Arthur and D. W. (after reading almost every single book in the Arthur series by Marc Brown) when their parents brought home their new baby sister. I remember telling my grandma, "I wish I could reach in to the book and hold her. She's so cute." And I remember being scared for Mitzi every time I read *Tell Me a Mitzi*, when she would take a taxi with her little brother, just the two of them, in the early morning hours on a New York City day.

Even though I don't attend Pajama Story Time anymore, and rarely even check out a book from the "library down the street," I still read stories in my little pink room before I sleep. Though the readings have changed and the stories have matured in difficulty and length, many of their themes and morals are drastically similar. And even those which are not really stories at all, they still make me feel and think, just on different levels, or about different things.

Sincerely,

Lindsay Rosenthal

High school student

⌇

> *My daughter is seven, and some of the other second-grade parents complain that their children don't read for pleasure. When I visit their homes, the children's rooms are crammed with expensive books, but the parents' rooms are empty. Those children do not see their parents reading, as I did every day of my childhood. By contrast when I walk into an apartment with books on the shelves, books on the bedside tables, books on the floor, and books on the toilet tank, then I know what I would see if I opened the door that says PRIVATE— GROWNUPS KEEP OUT: a child sprawled on the bed, reading.*
> —Anne Fadiman, *Ex Libris: Confessions of a Common Reader*

⌇

Dear Mr. Burke:

Your letter struck a spark in the mind and heart of a former teacher. First to my own life—books have brought the wealth of the universe, a realization of the intellectual achievements, the spiritual insights, the aesthetic pleasure, the ingenuity in all fields that our ancestors attained and passed on to us. Without the treasury stored up in libraries, we would be in the Stone Age.

In my classes I used to repeat an account of a woman whose identity I have unfortunately forgotten. She had been arrested for political reasons in Europe before World War II and subjected to solitary confinement for four years. On her release, her friends were amazed at her serenity and the clarity of her mind. When asked to account for this and to what she attributed her ability to have maintained her mental equilibrium, she said that she had no explanation but that she did know how she had passed her days. All her life, she explained, she had been a great reader and had traveled a great deal. Some days she would recall some book she had read and in her mind would go through the content of the book, live in its ambiance and work out her own reaction to it. Other days she would recall a particular place she had visited and relive the experience, imagining the sights and sounds, smells and feelings stored up in her memory. A mind filled with things outside herself had enabled her to people her loneliness and surmount her isolation.

Books can bring the whole world into our lives.

Sincerely,

Sister Christina Maria Weber

Teacher

⌒

A room without books in it is like a body without a soul.

—Cicero

⌒

Dear high school student 1-15-95
I think reading fells like angles
wispering to me. I love to read it is
very fun. by Chelsea L. Cameron

me

Dear Mr. Burke:

Your students might reflect on what has motivated and enriched my sixty-
seven-year-old life: books are man's best friend. Take me for an example. By the
time I was twenty-five years old, I had lost a brother in W.W.II, a father in a fish-
ing accident when I was four, a mother by heart attack, a cherished maiden aunt
only thirty-seven-years-old, and grandparents on both sides before I was six.

How else could I have survived without books, all kinds, history, poetry,
novels, and the Bible.

Enclosed is a book for you and your students.

Cordially,

Dr. Frank L. Keegan

Philosopher/historian

We read to know we are not alone.   —C. S. Lewis

Dear Students:

I always loved reading, but when I was in my 20s (forty years ago), I was
told that it was a "defense" presumably against the world. I stopped reading
for a while after that and then one day thought—Why not have a good
defense? And I started reading again.

A book that "entertained" me for at least a year in 1970 was *Black Lamb
& Grey Falcon* by Rebecca West. It is about a journey to Yugoslavia in
1937. At the time I heard about it, I was becoming interested in line dancing, the kind of dancing that is most common in Yugoslavia. I loved the
music and steps and wanted to learn more about people. It is a large book,
and I think I had read it twice because there was so much information in it,
when I had an opportunity to go to Yugoslavia for six weeks. It turned out
that although I knew a few people who were going to be there, I was really
traveling alone. I took the book along and it was almost a companion. I'll
give you a few instances.

Rebecca West talks in the book of the dramatic quality of individual
Yugoslavs—thus the people she met, even in a business setting, often

expressed themselves very personally to her. Only her long discussions with a nurse, in the preface, would have prepared me for seeing in a hotel one of the cleaning ladies cross the lobby crying and talking to herself while the person at the desk of the hotel paid no attention whatsoever. When is the last time you saw "personality" displayed in a hotel lobby?

In Belgrade on a Sunday, I went to Kalamegdan Park, which overlooks the confluence of two large rivers, the Sava and the Danube. It is the highest spot around. Everyone was enjoying the afternoon when suddenly it started to rain. Everyone ran. I don't think it is so upsetting to get wet, but the Yugoslavs did. So I ran, too, back to the hotel. I took out the book and read about a visit to the same park by Rebecca West and her husband, and it had rained that day, too, and the same thing had happened.

Then down south, in Macedonia, at Lake Ochrid, they stood on a bridge where a small river runs into the lake. One of them looked down and saw that at knee-level, there were bas-relief images carved in the bridge. They felt them and enjoyed them. When I went to Lake Ochrid, to that spot, I looked for the bridge and didn't see one like it with carvings. I asked at a hotel about the bridge and was told that when Bulgarians came over and occupied Macedonia in the Second World War, they had taken the bridge back with them to their country. Lake Ochrid is still very important to Bulgarians, who feel that area should be part of their country.

This trip was almost twenty-five years ago, and I have not opened the book very much in the intervening time. Now, with Yugoslavia in turmoil, I recently picked it up again and found, in the section on Bosnia-Herzegovina, feelings that account for much that is going on today. Lately I have been turning back to my "old friend," the book, to understand more about the world. One thing it illustrates is that regimes change, but people, personalities, are repeated.

Happy days!

Patricia Adelman

∽

> *There are only two or three human stories, and they go on repeating themselves as fiercely as if they had never happened before.*
> —Willa Cather

∽

Dear Mr. Burke:

I met a young lady on a visit to Finland in 1957. She was Swedish. About fifteen percent of people who live in Finland are Swedish, the rest are Finns. Their language is entirely different. Of course, a lot of people speak both languages plus English and German.

She didn't know any English and I didn't know any Swedish. I bought a Swedish grammar book, and a Swedish-English dictionary. After I arrived home, I began to study all by myself. I really didn't have much hope that I'd be able to learn the language. In school I took shop, and a lot of kids who took pre-college courses, which included a foreign language, had trouble learning a language.

At first, not much sank in, but gradually I began to catch on, then it became easier and easier.

On the job, when someone would say something, I would say it to myself in Swedish, and if I couldn't put it together, I'd look in my books at lunch time and at home.

So after four-and-a-half months, I wrote her a letter. It took me two-and-a-half hours. She answered and said she was surprised I had learned so quick. Of course I was far from being fluent. The next year I went to Finland and married her. At first, she hardly understood a word I said. She was a cute little redhead of about 45 kilos (100 lb.) and a nice figure so I had an incentive to learn.

I was fortunate to obtain an excellent grammar book. It was written by an instructor of Swedish at the University of London, otherwise I wouldn't have learned.

Enough gibberish for now.

Bill Hedstrom

P. S. I know my spelling is not so good, I get tired of looking in the dictionary —remember, I'm seventy-three.

⤳

She learned to read with you. She borrowed the books you read on tape out of the library, and followed what she heard, word by word and sentence by sentence. The tape machine couldn't handle all that constant switching on and off, and the rewinding and fast-forwarding. It kept breaking down and having to be repaired, and because that required permission, I finally found

out what Frau Schmitz was doing. She didn't want to tell me at first; when she also began to write, and asked me for a writing manual, she didn't try to hide it any longer. She was also just proud that she had succeeded, and wanted to share her happiness.
—Bernhard Schlink, *The Reader*

⤳

Do you know what Newton did? What made him famous? Neither did I until two years ago. But I'd studied (and received three degrees in) engineering and knew a great deal of math and physics. A book I borrowed from a library where I'd been a professor for almost 25 years then, told me on my first working visit back to my Ph.D. alma mater, UC Berkeley.

After reading bits of it, I bought my own copy and read every word.

Allen Klinger

Professor of engineering

⤳

During those ten years I read for reading's sake. I didn't do it to learn anything, though I found later on that I had learned a lot. I didn't read to prepare myself for a grown-up career, though I found later on that my ability to read helped me to make a living. I didn't read because anybody told me to. I didn't read to get ahead of anyone else, or to improve my marks in school. I read for the same reason we all like to open Christmas gifts. Each book was a surprise package stuffed with things I had no idea ever existed.

I grew bug-eyed over the miracle of language. How could a few punctuation marks plus words made out of twenty-six letters be put together so as actually to make (inside my head) people, animals, stories, landscapes, streets, towns, and even ideas? Here I was, a rather dull boy looking at an unopened book. Then within a short time the dull boy found he was entertained, amused, saddened, delighted, mystified, scared, dreamy, puzzled, astonished, held in suspense—all depending on what was in those ages. And sometimes he was bored—a perfectly reasonable thing to be and a good mood in which to develop judgment, for we can learn from what we dislike as well as from what we like.

My wish is that this set of books will give you some of these feelings—though I hope not boredom. It's good to get such feelings at an early age. They're never quite the same for the older reader. The older reader gets some of them, but more thinly, more weakly. He gets others, too, more complicated perhaps. But what he doesn't get in quite the same way is—surprise.

—Clifton Fadiman,
from his preface to *The World Treasury of Children's Literature*

Dear Students of Mr. Burke:

"Who am I, and what am I doing here?" Admiral Stockdale so eloquently inquired during last year's vice presidential debate. (I still think it was one of the most profound questions asked during the entire campaign!) I am Carol Karp, forty-six years old (same age as the president and many of your parents), a wife, a mother of one in college and one about to enter this fall, and an architect, a former student of Burlingame High School, a Cal graduate, and many other things, among the most important of which is that I am a life-long avid reader and lover of books.

I grew up in San Mateo when it was still a village and kids played baseball in the street and walked "downtown" in cut-offs and barefoot, and parents weren't afraid to let them. One of my most vivid memories was going to the library (they've since torn it down) by myself and selecting a huge stack of books to bring home. I thought it was wonderful that I could choose anything I wanted and looked forward to discovering what was between all those covers. I often read after "bed time" with a flash light, late into the night and thought this was about the most fun a person could have.

Books that stand out in my mind from those younger years (books that I will love all my life) are: *Heidi, Wizard of Oz, Anne of Green Gables, Little Women, The Five Little Peppers and How They Grew*, all the Nancy Drew mysteries, *Blue Willow*—so many others. Of course, I started with books long before then—picture books that were read to me when I was very young and which I gradually learned to read by myself. One of the best of those that I remember reading over and over was Virginia Burton's *The Little House*. It's still in print and I give it as gifts to young children because I loved it so and because I think it's one of the best books on the modern environment ever written—so simple but so true!

As I got older the books that affected me most strongly were: *The Diary of Anne Frank*, John Gunther's *Death Be Not Proud*, novels by the

Brontë sisters, so many more that I'd bore you with the list. Unfortunately, late into high school and all through college, I was too busy reading for school to read for pleasure. When I married and had small children to care for I despaired of ever reading a book again. I read children's books to them, but I didn't seem to have the uninterrupted time to read anything for myself but a short magazine article. If you want to know how fragmented a woman's life can become, read Anne Morrow Lindbergh's *A Gift from the Sea*! As the children got older and less dependent, I gradually got back into reading books, and I realize how much I missed during those "spouse" years. Reading has added a rich, imaginative inner life to the one I lead on the "outside." A good book leads you into the lives and times of others. It connects you to the emotional and intellectual currents of humanity. I look upon it as an almost religious experience. This probably sounds strange to someone who hasn't felt this way, but it's true and truly wonderful.

I feel a bit like someone making an acceptance speech at the Oscars—I don't want to forget to thank someone important! One summer about five years ago I decided to read *Grapes of Wrath*, which I hadn't read before. I enjoyed it so much that I decided to read *East of Eden*, both books by Steinbeck which I was only familiar with because they had been made into movies. Believe me, the books are better! After that I read everything Steinbeck wrote. I don't remember what else I did that summer—only that by the end of it, I had read all of Steinbeck's major works. What a thrill. I usually pick the reading I do by author. I will read anything Larry McMurtry writes (*Lonesome Dove* is my favorite) or anything Anne Tyler writes. I have recently discovered an author, Ferrol Samms, who wrote a trilogy about his boyhood in the South in the 1930s—absolutely wonderful, funny, insightful books that I think would be good reading for teenagers.

I'm tempted to try to put down every book I've read and enjoyed, but you would soon lose interest. My point is that reading is a great way to spend your life. Don't cheat yourself of this luxury. Nothing else is as meaningful—not TV, movies, computer games or hanging out with your friends. It's a way to discover the world and to discover yourself! Good luck to all of you!

Carol Karp

P. S. I can't leave out Willa Cather's *Death Comes to the Archbishop*, a book I just read recently—and loved!

⟋

Perhaps at every stage what we read is what we are, or what we are becoming, or desire.
    —Lynne Sharon Schwartz, *Ruined by Reading: A Life in Books*

December 17, 1992

Dear whoever,

I started taking myself seriously as a writer when I was 14, in high school in Houston, Texas. In school and in my family's house I felt I was in jail, and I wanted to be able to express myself freely with no one judging me because I was young.

In high school I was an outcast for being weird and also the school slut. There were moments when I was so depressed, I felt like no one ever would understand me. I didn't really have any friends except my books. My debate teacher gave me some poetry by Anne Sexton and Sylvia Plath, really violent, angry, warped poetry. It made a big difference to me that other women felt like I felt, and they wrote about it so powerfully. If they could write and be taken seriously, I knew I could too.

I got into collecting stuff from people I knew, poetry, essays, and cartoons, to put in a cheap xeroxed magazine. It seemed like in private everybody wrote or drew things, but they didn't have the confidence to think that their art was good, because it wasn't like the books we read in classes at school. They wrote like they talked, not in fancy correct English. They were afraid their feelings and problems were trivial. I wanted them to know that what they wrote was just as good and just as much "literature" as anybody else's writing. What was important was that they develop their own voice and their own style.

In school the books we read were always from 50 or a hundred years ago--- which was interesting, but seemed very remote from our lives.

Maybe at the very end of a semester a teacher would xerox a few stories or poems by someone who was alive now, writing in a more contemporary style, June Jordan or somebody like that. Nobody had to explain her writing to us- - -we didn't have to read any damn Cliff Notes! To my mind that is the best kind of literature, that people of our generation are writing, in OUR language, not in a dead language of 200, 100, even 50 years ago.

Literature is alive and growing. It is like a network of friends who only meet through writing. Someone writes a book and hopes that someone like you will read it and understand what they are saying. Their words might be important to you, even though you never meet them or talk to them.

Franz Kafka said that good literature should be an axe for the frozen sea inside of you. It shakes your feelings loose and helps you know who you are. I agree with this but I think that really good literature shows you that you yourself, not just some distant, genius author, are powerful enough to write something that other people will read. Your words can be an incredibly powerful and moving force. I encourage you to be active and do something whether it is writing, starting a band, or whatever. . . .just as long as you don't sit around waiting for life to happen to you. . . .

Liz Henry
alias Ms. Lizzard Thing

The City of Civilized Sex

Dear Fellow English Students and Comrades in Literature:

Hi. My name is Michael O'Leary. I am an itinerant housepainter, a semi-professional musician (aren't we all!), an erstwhile bartender, sometime student, perspiring youngish writer (sic), and a full-time and very avid reader. Reading is, quite simply, my drug of choice: It is the only smart drug I've ever encountered. Period. Not that reading should be taken as a drug, nor will it necessarily make one smart. Case in point: I am forty years of age, twice divorced, and about a dozen pounds overweight. Ah, but reading is the balm of Gilead.

In encouraging young people to read, I could dwell upon some obvious choices; to the hormone-fueled and libidinous I'd recommend the seductive and very quotable poetry of e. e. cummings and Walt Whitman, two very great Americans; there are the wildly diverse feminine viewpoints of such writers as Tillie Olsen, Amy Hemple, Katherine Anne Porter, Joyce Carol Oates, Flannery O'Connor, Tama Janowitz and Alice Walker, to name a few. To anyone I'd recommend the historical wit and wisdom of Mark Twain, the linguistic playfulness of Tom Robbins, the pragmatic cynicism of Vonnegut, the sensitive macho/bravado of Hemingway or the lyrical simplicity of Richard Braughtigan, and on and on and on. There is SO much to read . . . and so little time. . . . But you most likely don't want to hear someone of my debatable qualifications prate on about his literary tastes and heroes. I'll tell you about the one that "got me"—as a reader and a writer:

Ken Kesey's *Sometimes a Great Notion*.

I first read *Notion* in high school, and I guess it was, at first, the sheer verbal sinew and flights of language that drew me to it. Oh, it's a good story too, but just to read Kesey describe so simple a thing as a mile-long stretch of river can be a spiritual experience, an out of control holy rollercoaster, if you will. It must have taken at least two or three readings to really fathom most of the novel's subtleties, its character depth, subplots and its several moral conclusions (some of which, I suppose still elude me).

Anyway, since that first Eastertime fortnight, during the past twenty-four years, I must have read *Notion* a conservative dozen times (not to mention re-readings of favorite passages and episodes) and gone through almost that many volumes, what with lending, giving gifts, losing copies, and just flat wearing some of them out. Thank the gods for good used book stores!

Strangely enough, it wasn't until a few years later that I read Kesey's first novel and masterpiece *One Flew Over the Cuckoo's Nest* while serving a brief stint in city jail, in Mazatlan, Mexico. Talk about the perfect setting to read that novel. (But that's another story.)

So in conclusion I may as well crawl all the way out on this literary limb and state my opinion that, if there is such a beast, *Sometimes a Great Notion* is The Great American Novel. It has, to paraphrase William Faulkner on the "novel" in general, "the old verities and truths of the heart, the old universal truths lacking which any story is ephemeral and doomed—love and honor and pity and pride and compassion and sacrifice."

And how, you ask, has this book affected my life, what role has it played in my strutting and fretting about the stage? Well, I'd say in as many ways as a river has personalities, at least. Too cryptic? Too bad. Besides, you should check it out for yourselves. If you love to read already, you won't be disappointed; if you don't love to read, it just might be one of those rare, successful blind dates one hears of. Who knows? Check it out! Thanks for your time. . . .

Sincerely,

Michael O'Leary

House painter, bartender, musician

≈

The mystery of language was revealed to me. I knew then that "w-a-t-e-r" meant the wonderful cool something that was flowing over my hand. That living word awakened my soul, gave it light, joy, set it free.   —Helen Keller, *The Story of My Life*

≈

Dear Jim Burke:

I had taught school for twenty years, children grown and with their own families, when my husband became ill. Without the joy of the classroom, with depression from caring for a cancer-ridden husband, my nights were spent crying for that which I could not cure. Evil thoughts of death were my companion.

Then, one day, a true friend suggested I seek help from a clinical psychologist. I was shocked.

"Do you think I'm crazy?"

"No, but terribly disturbed," she put her hand on my shoulder. "Caring for a dying man twenty-four hours a day can be most trying."

I entered into a Jungian analysis, began to write my dreams, write my feelings. Childhood had been most painful and my feelings were acted out in stories of an abandoned child. When I had written a ream of stories, my analyst suggested I connect with the UCLA Extension and explore what they offered in writing.

The classes were exciting. I was a fifty-eight year-old woman in love with school again. I enrolled in every "writing for children" class offered. I joined a writing group where stories were shared, discussed, torn apart. I joined the Society of Children's Book Writers. I began to send out manuscripts to publishers of children's books.

The rejection letters poured in.

When UCLA announced their conference, Writers of the Pacific Rim, where Charlotte Zolotow, Children's Editor for Harper&Row would be the main speaker, I attended. At intermission, I approached Ms. Zolotow, explained my rejection letters and asked her advice.

"You just haven't found the right editor," she smiled.

The next day, *The Little Old Man and His Dreams* was mailed with a covering letter that began, "Remember me? I'm that middle aged woman who cornered you at UCLA."

One month later, a phone call came from Ms. Zolotow's office. "They were considering."

I continued to write, write, write.

Two months passed. I wrote, wrote, wrote. Another phone call. A contract was in the mail.

My first book was published six months before my husband died and on my 65th birthday.

The following year, *Buba Leah and Her Paper Children* was published.

This September, *Highlights for Children* magazine will carry my re-told Vietnamese story, "A Tall Tale."

Sarah Also Known As Hannah, the story of my mother's adventure on Ellis Island, 1910, will be in the bookstores soon.

Writing turned me around. It offered me a positive view of life and gave me the opportunity to see my stories in book form. Writing has allowed me to introduce my books to hundreds of children as I travel from school to school with my program, "A Birth of a Book."

Life is a joy! It depends how one looks at it.

Sharpen your pencils!

Best wishes,

Lillian Ross

Author

⌒

Dr. Seuss is remembered for the murder of Dick and Jane, which was a mercy killing of the highest order.   —Anna Quindlen

⌐

Dear Students:

I grew up on the streets of Brooklyn, New York. I went to a Catholic grammar school where I didn't do well. I was also raised in a family of abuse. Alcohol was the big problem. I started drinking young and never really got much done. Alcohol keeps you in a trance. My life changed very much by going back to school and reading books. Books have taken the place of alcohol. I now read about a book a week.

The most important thing I learn from a book is that we are all human beings. We must learn to love unconditionally. Everyone has shortcomings. That's what makes us human. Please don't make fun of people's looks and how they feel. Learn to get in touch with how you feel. It's OK to get angry, cry and to disagree with anyone. You must have your "feelings."

We are all "different" and we are all capable of much Love.

Kevin Burns

Insurance salesman

⌐

The women who came West were as strong as the men. I treat women with respect in my stories.   —Louis L'Amour

⌐

Mr. Burke:

I'm a helicopter test pilot and flight instructor for the U.S. Army at Los Alamitos, CA. I have over 7,000 hours of helicopter flight time, and I am currently the only female test pilot in the AH-1P Cobra helicopter. I am also the only female test pilot in the country in the OH-6A and UH-lM helicopters.

Books have *always* been important to me. I remember Nancy Drew as one of my early favorites. I've enjoyed so many books over the years, but the one that stands out for me is *The Search for Amelia Earhart* by Fred Goerner. I was in high school when I came across it.

I had always wanted to get into aviation and be a pilot, but the doors were closed to women in the 70s in the field of aviation. However, I remember reading about Amelia Earhart, her struggle and her around-the-world flight in 1937.

I could understand her frustrations and the excitement of her goals. Because of people like Amelia Earhart who dared to reach out, I believed I could accomplish my dream. And I did just that. Eight years after graduating high school, I became California's first woman aviator in the U.S. Army Reserves. Today, I continue with my dream by flying seven different types of helicopters.

Books have always been a part of my life. I have my own library in my home (mostly aviation and biographies) and my own encyclopedia set (something I had always wanted to own). I read every night before I go to sleep. Some of my favorite authors are: Dean Koontz, Tom Clancy, Clive Cussler, Dale Brown, Stephen Coontz, Scott Carpenter, Arthur C. Clarke, Ray Bradbury, Danielle Steel, and Larry McMurtry.

KEEP IN THOSE BOOKS—IT'S AN ADVENTURE!

Be Safe.

Geri Bowers

Helicopter pilot

⁀

> *My great-grandmother and Aunt Susie had been sent away to Carlisle Indian School in Pennsylvania, and both women had returned with a profound sense of the power of books. The laws were in books.*
> —Leslie Marmon Silko, *Yellow Woman and the Beauty of Spirit*

⁀

Dear Mr. Burke and Students:

We have to come ourselves to see the value of reading. Interestingly, some historical groups of people have never doubted the power of literacy. When writing was first invented, only the royal class were allowed to use it. Likewise, in medieval times, only priests were permitted the knowledge of writing and reading. Withholding this knowledge from the "common" people was a way of maintaining power over them. The priests were the only ones who could decipher important documents, record and transmit recorded information. Thus, they were able to appear terrifyingly wise to others, "calling forth" solar eclipses, for example, to frighten people when what they really were doing was reading astronomical records and predicting. More recently, people in our own country used the power of language to repress others. In the time of slavery, black people were not allowed to learn to read. Later, literacy tests was used to prevent blacks from registering to vote. Anti-abortion groups fought to keep doctors from giving information about abortion (written or oral) to people. You see, literacy is power. What could have happened if slaves learned to read or if women read about available health care?

Books not only transmit ideas, they provoke thought, compelling us to create our own ideas. Not surprisingly then, book banning is another way some people try to control others. If young people read *Catcher in the Rye*, the argument goes, they may try to emulate the rough-talking, authority-questioning, independent-minded hero. If they read something we disagree with, they may develop independent—i.e., contrary—notions. Nobel-prize winning author Gabriel Garcia Marquez was restricted by our government in terms of his visiting New York to promote his latest book; it seems our government feared the ideas Garcia Marquez could disseminate through his writing (he is a friend of Fidel Castro's).

Reading, and reading lots of varied stuff, empowers people, makes us smarter, more articulate, harder to take advantage of (thanks to reading, I know about eclipses and personal rights, among other things). But, it takes a mind that has through reading exposed itself to human literature to know that; ah, there's the rub. I realize that I'm writing about the value of reading books and the value of literacy in general. I've done so because one leads to the other and back again; reading makes us literate, which makes us want to read some more. Once we reach that point, there's no stopping us in what we can think or achieve.

I'll stop myself, finally, with a quote from Alice Walker's *The Temple of My Familiar*. "Keep in mind always the present you are constructing. It should be the future you want."

Sincerely,

Diana Acevedo

Writer

⪜

Growing up with five brothers taught me that it's good to be the guy telling the story after the lamp gets broken.
                    —Jon Scieszka, picture book writer

⪜

Dear Mr. Burke:

My name is Mariam Lubet. I am forty-five years old. I teach first grade. I spend most of my days teaching literacy to my class.

Part of my career choice was based on my love of books and my desire to transfer that love to others.

My love of reading came from my father. He was an immigrant. English was his second language. He loved to go to the library and read newspapers.

I have always loved to read. I have been reading my whole life. I can not go to sleep at night unless I read.

A few years ago my class wrote letters to Roald Dahl. He answered. I'm enclosing a copy of his letter for you and your students.

Sincerely,

Mariam Lubet

Elementary school teacher

4th June 1985

    Hello gorgeous Miriam and all the clever children in the first grade class. Thank you for sending me your super letters.

    May I tell you why it is important for children to read good books? If, when you are young, you read just one book that is so funny and exciting that you fall in love with it, then there is a good chance that this little love affair with a single book will convince you that reading is terrific fun, and this experience is almost sure to lead you on to reading other good books. Then, with luck, you will become a reader of books for the rest of your life. An adult reader of books has a terrific advantage over the non-reader. Sooner or later, all of you are going to suffer some kind of loneliness or illness, and the comfort you will get from being "a book-reader" as opposed to just a silly television watcher will be enormous.

                With love from,

Roald Dahl

⤳

Dear Mr. Burke:

I began escaping into books when I was pretty young. It wasn't that I was a bookworm or anything, I just needed to escape into my own world sometimes. A lot.

I came from what they now call a dysfunctional family. I called it messed up. My father was an alcoholic, and my mother would sometimes join in the festivities. There would be fighting, parties, waking up to strangers on the way to the kitchen in the morning. But I would still get up, get dressed, and get myself to school.

So I escaped to books. Sure we had a television, but it's not easy to carry a television when you run away. It was easier to grab a book and just find a peaceful, quiet spot. Then I could really be a kid: I could retreat into my imagination and have the kind of adventures I could only dream about.

First it was books like *James and the Giant Peach* and *Charlie and the Chocolate Factory* or *The Adventures of Pippi Longstocking*. Now Pippi, she was really cool. She was so independent and she had all these magic powers to help her out of jams.

Soon I graduated to more "mature" reading: *A Tree Grows in Brooklyn*, *To Kill a Mockingbird*, *The Pearl*, and *The Good Earth*. The world around me was becoming so much wider and more interesting, and yet, physically I hadn't moved an inch.

Books really carried me through some trying times. They helped me understand that there was a life beyond what I knew; that there were exotic lands, mischievous children, charming princesses, and families that loved each other; that life was a joy to be experienced, not just a pain to be endured. Books became surrogate parents that taught me that learning, growing and exploring is important.

I never really knew where my love for reading would lead me in life, I just knew it would always be there—like a good friend. As I look back, it gave me a love for knowledge that led me to college where I majored in Business and Television/Film. As a career, I always knew I loved the creative fields, but I wasn't really an actor, singer, dancer type. So I really didn't know where I would fit in. But my love for books and knowledge lead me exactly to where I should be. I am now a script reader (development person) for a producer in the film industry. I earn a living reading about those same types of adventures, and being one of the team that decides if a particular book, script or idea would make a good movie or television show.

I am so thankful that I developed a love for reading at an early age, because most of the successful people I meet in life (whether in the entertainment business or not) are so well read, and so sharp, that without my reading background, I would never be able to keep up. Most successful people I talk to agree that learning is a lifelong process that doesn't just end with high school or college. Business people, performers, writers and other professionals, I find are constantly reading newspapers, books and magazines to keep up with new ideas, trends and opportunities. There are many skills in this world that are so specialized and precise (like brain surgery) that it cannot be learned by just anyone. But the ability to read well is a skill that everyone can develop and count on as a major building block on their road to success.

M.G.

Script developer

⌐

> *So to hold a book was always to arrest time, a way to stay the world. To hold a book was to hold steady what I could not.*
> —Robert Olmstead, "On the Way to the Books," from *The Most Wonderful Books: Writers on Discovering the Pleasures of Reading*

⌐

Dear Students of Jim Burke,

Writing poems, short stories, & plays have been important for me in my life. When I was growing up I felt invisible. I never thought my parents really knew who I was. So I had fantasies of becoming famous, so they would have to notice me. At first I wanted to be a famous baseball player, like Mickey Mantle. But after I kept striking out at the plate, I decided to be a famous writer. So being a writer is essential to me, because it means that I haven't betrayed my dreams. Nowadays I don't need to be famous, but I need to write.

Also I always said the best things to people after they were gone. What I mean by that is that after I hung up the phone, or after a friend would leave, I would still keep talking to that person in my mind, even though the person was no longer there. That's why I need to write, because my mind is like a radio that I can't shut off, it keeps talking & talking, and by writing down my thoughts, I'm finally able to shut it off for a while.

In college I took a course with the writer, Ralph Ellison. We had to read many books, & I remember one paragraph very well that I read. The author said that you think differently when you write. I found that to be true. When I'm thinking to myself my thoughts are all jumbled. But when I start to write them down, they become clearer.

And just like Mr. Burke, I am also a teacher. So don't try to be bad in his class. I work in an elementary school with students who have special needs. That's all I have to say for now. I hope Mr. Burke doesn't find any spelling or grammar mistakes in this letter, but that's the chance you take when you become a writer. Enclosed is a poem that an artist, who I never met, illustrated for me.

Sincerely,

Hal Sirowitz

Teacher/writer

Dear Mr. Burke and Students:

My name is Jimmy White, I'm twenty-nine years old and a psychiatric case manager for a nonprofit agency that provides mental health services for the mentally disabled. I'm writing to you because I want to let you know how important books and reading are to me. When I was a child, my family was extremely poor and as a result we had to move from town to town so my parents could find work. By the time I was 13, I had lived in 22 different places! This constant moving meant that I was always "The new kid on the block" and therefore always felt ostracized. I never felt like I belonged anywhere. Forming friendships was difficult, especially when the threat of moving so often loomed over my head; it's hard to get close to someone when you know that you will probably leave them.

Given these circumstances, it's no wonder I hated my world and thus began reading. Reading offered me a healthy escape into other worlds. I say "a healthy escape" because we all know how many other forms of escape there are that are unhealthy: drugs, for example. Anyway, I found that through books I could enter other times, existences, realities, etc. I could become the hero or the hero's companion. Some of my favorite books then were books by Edgar Rice Burroughs. He's most famous for creating Tarzan, but he also wrote some fantastic science fiction series that are quick and easy to read. Other favorites of mine were *A Separate Peace* by John Knowles, *The Collector* by John Fowles, *Salem's Lot* by Stephen King (I couldn't sleep for two weeks after reading this one!), *The Hobbit* [and *Lord of the Rings*] trilogy by Tolkien, *Watership Down* by [Richard] Adams, *1984* and *Animal Farm* by George Orwell, *A Tale of Two Cities* by Charles Dickens, *Robinson Crusoe* by Daniel Defoe, *Slaughterhouse Five* by Kurt Vonnegut Jr. and *The Little House on the Prairie* series by Laura Ingalls Wilder.

These books were an important part of my growing up and I'll cherish the memories I have of staying up well past my bedtime because I couldn't put the book down on various occasions. Today reading is one of my favorite pastimes. I started keeping a book diary in 1990 and each year I try to read more books than the previous year. Let me make a suggestion: If your world is scary or lonely or confusing or overwhelming, don't try suicide or drugs, try a book instead. It's a much more rewarding, enriching wonderful experience than those self-destructive

ways (and believe me, I'm speaking from personal experience!) I hope
this doesn't sound preachy because it's coming from the heart. I sincerely wish the best for each of you.

Yours truly,

Jimmy White

Psychiatric case manager

⤳

*Find the most comfortable position: seated, stretched out, curled
up, or lying flat. . . . Stretch your legs, go ahead and put your feet
on a cushion, on two cushions, on the arms of the sofa, on the
wings of the chair, on the coffee table, on the desk, on the piano,
on the globe. Take your shoes off first. . . . Adjust the light so you
don't strain your eyes. Do it now, because once you're absorbed
in reading there will be no budging you. . . . Try to foresee anything that might interrupt your reading. Cigarettes within reach,
if you smoke, and the ashtray. Anything else? Do you have to
pee? All right, you know best.*

—Italo Calvino, *If on a winter's night a traveler*

⤳

Dear Mr. Burke and Students:

One day, while flying over a distant country, I realized I did not know my
younger sister. I had left home when she was twelve. She was still a child to
me; I had no idea who or what I was to her. I wanted to tell her who I was
and how I saw the world; I wanted to know the same from her. I didn't
want to write for hours or days, and I didn't know when I would see her
again, or if she'd want to have the kind of talk I imagined. How was I to
communicate so much in the short space of a letter?

I thought about books . . . the books I'd read that had an impact on me;
the ones that I'd read and said "Yes! That's what I mean!" Books that spoke
of a world far different than the one I grew up in; that expressed a vision;
that might help her understand why I was living a life so different than the
one our parents mapped out for me; those were the books I'd tell her about.

"Read this!" I wrote. "Read this if you want to understand some of what I'm talking about!"

For your purposes, what books I urged her to read might not be important. Your students don't know me and don't need to know me. The books I gave to my sister when I got back to the U.S. were *Island*, by Aldous Huxley, and *The Dispossessed*, by Ursula K. Le Guin. Both books develop utopian societies; between them, they encompassed much of my vision of a possible world. Both societies were real in the sense that they dealt not with the absence of conflict in a perfect world, but with the conflicts that arose in those societies and how they were handled.

As novels they could traffic in political, social, and economic ideas without being dry and boring like a textbook or political tract. As novels they could propose "dangerous" ideas without themselves being dangerous. We all know that novels are "entertainment."

Children's books have also been important to me. I started reading children's books as an adult. *The Annotated Alice*, an edition of Lewis Carroll's *Alice in Wonderland* and *Through the Looking Glass*, with notes by Martin Gardner, makes the Alice books much more than I thought they were and helps to explain why a mathematician was writing children's books. Then I discovered books written for children by the playwright Eugene Ionesco and the poets e.e. cummings and Carl Sandburg. I read stories on a radio program for children and spent hours each week in the children's section of a local bookstore, searching for exciting and unusual books to read to the kids on the air.

Now I've entered a new phase. I'm reading literature from Latin America and the Spanish language is coming alive for me in new ways. I'm realizing how little Spanish I know even though I can talk to people, and learning more of the beauty of the language as I see how things can be expressed in Spanish and how that's different than a simple translation. At the same time as I see the differences in the language, I see the sameness in the human condition. Reading *Los Fantoches* by Carlos Solorzano, I see the same questions about what it means to be a human being that I wonder about in English. Reading *Muerte constante mas alla del amor*, by Gabriel Garcia Marquez, I see a master of his language talking about the feelings of alienation and loneliness that we all must face, and the sham of politics in a system not as different from ours as we'd like to think. Reading in a second language both enlarges my world and brings it closer.

I didn't think I'd need a second page. When I started to write this, I was just going to write about giving books to my little sister. The other parts just sorta came up.

Sincerely,

Steve Larkin

∽

Know something, sugar? Stories only happen to the people who can tell them.   —Allan Gurganus

∽

Hello, Mr. Burke . . . and students:

Shall try not to set your literacy teachings back too far . . . and punctuation rules and stuff like that there . . . but I've been running a cattle ranch for 40 years and one does get a bit rusty around the edges.

Oh, I read a lot . . . don't get me wrong . . . but I read for relaxation now, for mind "unwinding" at the end of the day and no longer to acquire knowledge that I'm durn sure I'll never put to use. Or even to read to broaden my knowledge of places I've never been to or are likely to see. Bein' 69 does that to many a person . . . not every person but a lot of 'em. . . .

Y'see . . . a livestock operation, a cattle ranch, is sort of a demanding thing. There's always a fence to look after . . . maybe fix . . . what with thirty miles of it around and criss-crossing the place. Some of the wood posts have been in since it was built some 70 years ago. Dry out here . . . and the posts are cedar . . . but they're beginning to give way, finally. And there's hay to put up and then one moves the durn stuff to the feeding corrals and pretty soon it is winter and you gotta feed every day and then spring and calving time and then summer comes around again and it's time to hay, etc., etc., etc. . . . Just a small operation . . . what you would probably term a mom and pop operation . . . for we had sheep up until 40 years ago and it was too much hassle what with sheepherders and hired help at lambing time and a sheep being the most exasperating, dumbest thing ever put on this green— sometimes, even out here—earth.

But as a kid, growing up in the country . . . until high school the country schools had seven to maybe fifteen kids in all the seven or eight grades, one teacher for all . . . well, if one was ever to learn what it was like on the "outside" you had to read a book. When you get around a team and wagon or horseback, your horizons are kinda limited . . . especially in the winter time. Summer school . . . eight months of the year, stay home December, January, February, March. Come time I was of school age, my mother, brother, and I came down from the sheep ranch which was just seven miles south of the Canadian border and took over a country store and post office. Half mile walk to school. That one year. Next year, they consolidated three rural schools—the homesteaders were pulling out in bunches as it was in the Depression years of the '30s so they didn't have as many students to teach. Two mile walk—each way—when a car didn't come along but part of the time, we had a saddle horse to ride. Healthy . . . and tiring, didn't need a whole lot of parental urging to go to bed at night. . . .

Had a small community lending library in one corner of the store and I guess I read every book in it. And magazines, we subscribed to a few, and there was a lot of swapping of those old paper-pulp westerns and detective magazines among the neighbors year around. And there were two other sources of reading material . . . there being three different mail routes from rural towns that met at Genevieve, the store-post office and in those days the farmers all milked some cows and sold cream to the creameries. The mail carriers took it down to the railroad in five-gallon cans and it was shipped along and the cans came back via carrier also. They had been washed out and all, but to soak up the moisture and keep them from rusting inside, the creameries would, after drying them, toss in a couple of paper pulp magazines to help soak up the last moisture. Boy, when I discovered this, I had it made!! If, that is, the people weren't waiting there for their cans when the mail came. One had to be a fast reader because if I didn't chuck two magazines in the can when I removed the originals, there would be the dickens to pay. Not only might the cans rust, the other folks looked forward to getting a couple free magazines also. The other source of reading material . . . the drug stores in town sold the magazines, nickel, dime, sometimes two bits, and those they could not sell, they could return for a refund and all they had to do was tear the front covers off and send them in. So you could buy a bundle of assorted reading material . . . comic book or two, lots of detective stories, some westerns, some real literary magazines, some movie mags, whole bunch of stuff for two bits. Dad had one or two sheepherders up north to keep supplied with reading material . . . sheepherders having lots of spare time on the better days . . . and I got to pick through the bundles when he came from town.

No electricity out that far. Poor radio reception and radios required bat-
teries that were always running down so that was not much of a means of
getting the word. So it was mostly reading. Folks got it made . . . in that way
. . . these days.

Reading won't ever go out of style. Books won't. As yet, there is no way
to turn a TV program back a page or two to view again if you don't quite
"get it." Video is something else . . . if you have unlimited numbers of cas-
settes around, if you got all the time to search through them, you can do
quite well. On the current status of it, what it looks like today. . . . But what
about how it was, what about the history of this place, that place, this
development, this industry? Here you can do best with books, with ency-
clopedias. Way better . . . by far the best way. One with any amount of natural curiosity about how things come about, evolved . . . you have to turn
to the printed page. The ability to do so easily means a lot. It means a whole
hell of a lot when your turn comes to go out looking for employment.
Yeah, sure . . . you can call up any amount of information by punching the
proper computer keys. But presently, you still have to be able to read it.
Maybe now, maybe soon, they'll have computers that talk to you and tell
you what you want to know. But the printed page, my friends, is a long
ways from becoming obsolete. Learn how to get familiar with them and
their contents. . . .

Now me, new knowledge I don't really need much at sixty-nine. Got the
cows, got the ranch, the kids got through college in good shape, I figure just
to kind of ride it out the remaining years. And I imagine I can. But for you
. . . with much of life yet ahead of you, a job, then a career, perhaps commit-
ments that won't allow you to travel, to see the world, with the natural
curiosity of youth, books will fill in where TV and videos kind of hit
around the edges.

Had it to do all over again, I'd maybe do it about the same and even
wind up here. Country living, boarding out for the high school years,
armed combat in World War 2, four years of college, an honors graduate
(changed from engineering to agriculture in the process) . . . well, I had my
options and one of the reasons I had 'em was because I was mighty familiar
with the printed page and the words on it. Could have taught, could have
gone into agricultural research, gone with banks or the government agencies as an ag rep man, there was opportunity. I won't say it all started with
the Genevieve Community Lending Library or those milk-can pulp maga-

zines or the variety of literary offerings in the two-bit sheepherder bundles. But everything has gotta start someplace . . . we all know that.

Good Luck,

John H. Barton

Cattle rancher

⟳

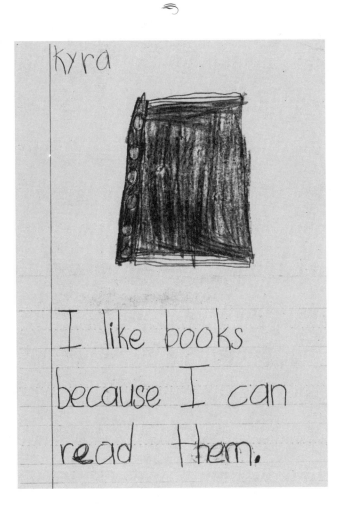

APPENDIX A

What We Read:
The I HEAR AMERICA READING
List of Lists

⌒

Any book list is an argument, an invitation to begin a conversation. These lists will prove helpful to the extent that you argue with them, thinking in the process why some other book or author should or should not be on this list. I limited the lists to ten (with one exception) for the simple reason that you cannot create any such thing as a complete list; better to pick a fight and let you figure it out on your own.

The only evidence I will offer as to the quality of these books is the credibility of those who nominated them. CATENet, an on-line round table I moderate for English teachers, was a source of many ideas and titles. My students, both past and present, were essential contributors, as were my wife, colleagues, and even strangers sitting next to us in malls while my wife and I argued over whether or not to include *A Wrinkle in Time.*

These lists and others are also available on my Web site (www.englishcompanion.com) and will be supplemented as new ideas come to me. The conversations that yielded these lists were among the most intriguing parts of the process as they challenged everyone involved to think not only why we read certain books but why, for example, one might think William Faulkner's books far exceed the importance of Ken Kesey's or why Roald Dahl's *Charlie and the Chocolate Factory* is a wonderful book but *The BFG* has to be on the list (according to my son). After reading this book and the lists below, why not go to the Web site and submit your own lists? Join the conversation.

TEN BOOKS FOR PEOPLE WHO THINK THE WORLD IS ABSURD

1. *The Basketball Diaries*, Jim Carroll
2. *Bonfire of the Vanities*, Tom Wolfe
3. *Cat's Cradle*, Kurt Vonnegut, Jr.
4. *Catch-22*, Joseph Heller
5. *Even Cowgirls Get the Blues*, Tom Robbins
6. *Hitchhiker's Guide to the Galaxy* (and other books in the trilogy), Douglass Adams
7. *One Flew Over the Cuckoo's Nest*, Ken Kesey
8. *Satanic Verses*, Salman Rushdie
9. *Scoop*, Evelyn Waugh
10. *V*, Thomas Pynchon

TEN BOOKS FOR THE ADVENTUROUS

1. *Hatchet*, Gary Paulsen
2. *Into Thin Air*, Jon Krakauer
3. *The Mosquito Coast*, Paul Theroux
4. *The Perfect Storm*, Sebastian Junger
5. *The Right Stuff*, Tom Wolfe
6. *Seven Summits*, Dick Bass and Frank Wells (with Rick Ridgeway)
7. *Shooting the Boh: A Woman's Voyage down the Wildest River in Borneo*, Tracy Johnston
8. *Tracks: A Woman's Solo Trek Across 1,700 Miles of Australian Outback*, Robyn Davidson
9. *Travelers' Tales: The Best of Travelers' Tales*, Larry Habegger (editor)
10. *Treasure*, Clive Cussler

TEN BOOKS TO READ ALOUD IN THE CAR WHILE TRAVELING

1. *Baseball and Summer Squash*, Don Graves
2. *Dispatches*, Michael Herr
3. *The Education of Little Tree*, Forrest Carter
4. *Fear and Loathing in Las Vegas*, Hunter S. Thompson
5. *James and the Giant Peach*, Roald Dahl
6. *The Legacy of Conquest: The Unbroken Past of the American West*, Patricia Nelson Limerick
7. *Life on the Mississippi*, Mark Twain
8. *Little House on the Prairie*, Laura Ingalls Wilder
9. *Rising Tide*, John Barry
10. *A Summer Life*, Gary Soto

TEN BOOKS WORTH READING ALOUD TO YOUR CHILDREN

1. *A Child's Christmas in Wales*, Dylan Thomas
2. *Fairy Tales* (Pantheon series)
3. *Goodnight Moon*, Margaret Wise Brown
4. *Green Eggs and Ham*, Dr. Seuss
5. *Little House on the Prairie*, Laura Ingalls Wilder
6. *Polar Express*, Chris Van Allsburg

7. *The Stinky Cheese Man*, John Scieszka
8. *Taxi Dog*, Debra Barracca
9. *The Velveteen Rabbit*, Margery Williams
10. *Where the Sidewalk Ends*, Shel Silverstein

TEN BOOKS ABOUT AMERICA

1. *American Dreams*, Studs Terkel
2. *Blue Highways*, William Least Heat Moon
3. *Citizen Soldiers*, Stephen Ambrose
4. *A Different Mirror: A History of Multicultural America*, Ron Takaki
5. *Jasmine*, Bharati Mukherjee
6. *The Jungle*, Upton Sinclair
7. *Lies My Teacher Told Me*, Gerald Eskelin
8. *Revising America*, Frances Fitzgerald
9. *Saturday Night In America*, Susan Orlean
10. *The Way We Never Were: American Families and the Nostalgia Trap*, Stephanie Coontz

TEN BOOKS ABOUT BOOKS

1. *Ex Libris: Confessions of a Common Reader*, Anne Fadiman
2. *Genesis: As It Is Written*, David Rosenberg
3. *The Gutenberg Elegies: The Fate of Reading in the Electronic Age*, Sven Birkerts
4. *Great Books*, David Denby
5. *A History of Reading*, Alberto Manguel
6. *How Reading Changed My Life*, Anna Quindlen
7. *Imagining Characters*, A. S. Byatt and Iris Sordre
8. *The Most Wonderful Books: Writers on Discovering the Pleasures of Reading*, Michael Dorris and Emilie Buchwald
9. *The rise of the image, the fall of the word*, Mitchell Stephens
10. *Ruined by Reading*, Lynne Schwartz

TEN BOOKS OF BOOKLISTS

1. *The Book Group Book*, Ellen Slezak
2. *Books for a Small Planet: A Multicultural-Intercultural Bibliography for Young English Language Learners*, Dorothy S. Brown
3. *500 Great Books by Women: A Reader's Guide*, Erica Bauermeister, et al.
4. *Great Books for Girls: More than 600 Books to Inspire Today's Girls and Tomorrow's Women*, Kathleen Odean
5. *A Lifetime Reading Plan*, Clifton Fadiman
6. *New York Public Library's Books of the Century*, ed. E Diefendorf
7. *The 100 Most Influential Books Ever Written: The History of Thought from Ancient Times to Today*, Martin Seymour-Smith
8. *The Reading Group Book: The Complete Guide to Starting and Sustaining a Reading Group, with Annotated Lists of 250 Titles for Provocative Discussion*, Davis Laskin and Holly Hughes

9. *Strong Souls Singing: African American Books for Our Daughters and Our Sisters* and *Spirited Minds: African American Books for Our Sons and Our Brothers,* edited by Archie Givens.
10. *The Western Canon,* Harold Bloom

TEN BOOKS A TEENAGE BOY WOULD WANT TO READ

1. *Always Running,* Luis Rodriguez
2. *Dogsong,* Gary Paulsen
3. *Enders Game,* Orson Scott Card
4. *Lord of the Rings,* J. R. R. Tolkien
5. *Makes Me Want to Holler,* Nathan McCall
6. *A River Runs Through It,* Norman Maclean
7. *Rule of the Bone,* Russell Banks
8. *The Things They Carried,* Tim O'Brien
9. *This Boy's Life,* Tobias Wolff
10. *Way Past Cool,* Jess Mowry

TEN NEW CHILDREN'S BOOKS ANYONE WOULD LOVE (BUT KIDS ESPECIALLY)

1. *Amanda Pig and Her Best Friend Lollipop,* Jean Van Leeuwen
2. *The Animal Rescue Club,* John Himmelman
3. *Bathtime for Biscuit,* Alyssa Capucilli
4. *Bugs, Beetles, and Butterflies,* Harriet Ziefert
5. *Can You Guess Where We're Going?,* Elvira Woodruff
6. *Forest,* Laura Godwin
7. *Marianthe's Story,* Aliki
8. *Mr. Putter & Tabby Toot the Horn,* Cynthia Rylant
9. *Sam the Zamboni Man,* James Stevenson
10. *Thank You, Mr. Falker,* Patricia Polacco

TEN BOOKS WE SHOULD ALL READ BEFORE CHILDHOOD ENDS

1. *The BFG,* Roald Dahl
2. *The Box Car Children,* Gertrude Chandler Warner
3. *Charlotte's Web,* E. B. White
4. *Green Eggs and Ham,* Dr. Seuss
5. *Indian in the Cupboard,* Lynne Reid Banks
6. *The Lion, The Witch, and the Wardrobe,* C. S. Lewis
7. *Little House on the Prairie,* Laura Ingalls Wilder
8. *The Secret Garden,* Frances Hodgson Burnett
9. *The Wind in the Willows,* Kenneth Grahame
10. *A Wrinkle in Time,* Madeline L'Engle

TEN BOOKS ABOUT CULTURES

1. *Balkan Ghosts: A Journey Through History,* Robert Kaplan
2. *From Beirut to Jerusalem,* Thomas L. Friedman
3. *Genesis (Memory of Fire Trilogy, Part 1),* Eduardo H. Galeano

4. *The Gift of the Jews: How a Tribe of Desert Nomads Changed the Way Everyone Thinks and Feels*, Thomas A. Cahill
5. *How the Irish Saved Civilization: The Untold Story of Ireland's Heroic Role from the Fall of Rome to the Rise of Medieval Europe*, Thomas A. Cahill
6. *India: A Million Mutinies Now*, V. S. Naipaul
7. *My Traitor's Heart: A South African Exile Returns to Face His Country, His Tribe, and His Conscience*, Rian Milan
8. *Pictures from the Water Trade: Adventures of a Westerner in Japan*, John David Morley
9. *Tales of the City*, Armistead Maupin
10. *A Turn in the South*, V. S. Naipaul

TEN BOOKS FOR A DESERT ISLAND

1. *The Annotated Alice*, Lewis Carroll
2. *Collected Works of Shakespeare* (Harold Bloom's choice)
3. *The Divine Comedy* (Pinsky translation), Dante Alighieri
4. *Finnegans Wake*, James Joyce
5. *The Histories*, Herodotus
6. *King James Bible* (William Faulkner's choice)
7. *The Odyssey*, Homer (Fagles translation)
8. *Waiting for Godot*, Samuel Beckett
9. *Walden*, Henry David Thoreau
10. *Wherever You Go, There You Are*, Jon Kabar-Zinn

TEN ESSENTIAL BOOKS ABOUT EDUCATION

1. *American Education (3-volume history)*, Lawrence A. Cremin
2. *Cultivating Humanity: A Classical Defense of Reform in Liberal Education*, Martha Nussbaum
3. *The End of Education*, Neil Postman
4. *Horace's Hope: What Works for the American High School*, Theodore Sizer
5. *Hunger of Memory: The Education of Richard Rodriguez*, Richard Rodriguez
6. *The Padeia Proposal*, Mortimer Adler
7. *Releasing the Imagination*, Maxine Greene
8. *Savage Inequalities*, Jonathon Kozol
9. *School Girls: Young Girls, Self-Esteem, and the Confidence Gap*, Peggy Orenstein
10. *The Schools We Need and Why We Don't Have Them*, E. D. Hirsch

TEN BEST FILMS THAT BEGAN AS BOOKS

1. *Apocalypse Now*, Joseph Conrad (from *Heart of Darkness*)
2. *The Color Purple*, Alice Walker
3. *Cry, the Beloved Country*, Alan Paton
4. *The Dead*, James Joyce
5. *The English Patient*, Michael Ondaatje
6. *Last of the Mohicans*, James Fenimore Cooper
7. *The Name of the Rose*, Umberto Eco
8. *One Flew Over the Cuckoo's Nest*, Ken Kesey
9. *A River Runs Through It*, Normal Maclean
10. *To Kill a Mockingbird*, Harper Lee

Ten Books About the Future

1. *Being Digital*, Nicholas Negroponte
2. *Brave New World*, Aldous Huxley
3. *Children of Men*, P. D. James
4. *The Earthsea Trilogy*, Ursula Le Guin
5. *The Giver*, Lois Lowry
6. *Handmaid's Tale*, Margaret Atwood
7. *Kindred*, Octavia Butler
8. *Left Behind*, Rim LaHaye and Jerry B. Jenkins
9. *The Popcorn Report: Faith Popcorn on the Future of Your Company, Your World, and Your Life*, Faith Popcorn
10. *Snow Crash*, Neal Stephenson

Twenty Books a Teenage Girl Would Want to Read

1. *Anne of Green Gables*, L. M. Montgomery
2. *Anywhere But Here*, Mona Simpson
3. *Bastard Out of Carolina*, Dorothy Allison
4. *Betsey Brown*, Ntozake Shange
5. *Black Ice*, Lorene Cary
6. *The Bluest Eye*, Toni Morrison
7. *Bridge to Terabithia*, Katherine Paterson
8. *Coffee Will Make You Black*, April Sinclair
9. *Dharma Girl*, Chelsea Cain
10. *Divine Secrets of the Ya-Ya Sisterhood*, Rebecca Wells
11. *Ellen Foster*, Kaye Gibbons
12. *Forever*, Judy Blume
13. *Girl Interrupted*, Suzanne Kaysen
14. *How the Garcia Girls Lost Their Accent*, Julie Alvarez
15. *Jane Eyre*, Charlotte Brontë
16. *Joy Luck Club*, Amy Tan
17. *Reviving Ophelia*, Mary Pipher
18. *She's Come Undone*, Wally Lamb
19. *A Tree Grows in Brooklyn*, Betty Smith
20. *When I Was Puerto Rican*, Esmeralda Santiago

Ten Recommendations for The Great American Novel

(Note: Everyone who nominated a title said
"The Great American Novel" has yet to be written.)

1. *Absalom! Absalom!*, William Faulkner
2. *The Adventures of Huckleberry Finn*, Mark Twain
3. *Beloved*, Toni Morrison
4. *Bonfire of the Vanities*, Tom Wolfe
5. *The Grapes of Wrath*, John Steinbeck
6. *The Invisible Man*, Ralph Ellison
7. *Moby Dick*, Herman Melville

8. *Sometimes a Great Notion*, Ken Kesey
9. *To Kill a Mockingbird*, Harper Lee
10. *Uncle Tom's Cabin*, Harriet Beecher Stowe

TEN BOOKS TO HELP HIGH SCHOOL ENGLISH TEACHERS TRIUMPH

1. *Creating Writers*, Vicki Spandel and Richard Stiggins
2. *Curriculum as Conversation*, Arthur Applebee
3. *Daybook of Critical Reading and Writing (Series: 9–12)*,
   Fran Claggett, Louann Reid, Ruth Vinz
4. *The English Teacher's Companion: A Complete Guide to Classroom, Curriculum, and the Profession*, Jim Burke
5. *Literature as Exploration, Fifth Edition*, Louise Rosenblatt
6. *A Measure of Success*, Fran Claggett
7. *Questioning the Author: An Approach to Enhancing Student Engagement with Text*, Isabel L. Beck, Margaret G. McKeown, Rebecca L. Hamilton, and Linda Kucan
8. *Reading Engagement: Motivating Readers Through Integrated Instruction*, John T. Guthrie and Alan Wigfield (editors)
9. *What a Writer Needs*, Ralph Fletcher
10. *Write for College: A Student Handbook*, Patrick Sebranek, Verne Meyer, and Dave Kemper

TEN HISTORICAL NOVELS YOU'LL LOVE

1. *Burr*, Gore Vidal
2. *Dead Man's Walk*, Larry McMurtry
3. *The Eight*, Katherine Neville
4. *Gospel*, Wilton Barnhardt
5. *Hawaii*, James Michener
6. *Killer Angels*, Michael Shaara
7. *Midnight's Children*, Salman Rushdie
8. *The Name of the Rose*, Umberto Eco
9. *Schindler's List*, Thomas Keneally
10. *Trinity*, Leon Uris

TEN BOOKS TO MAKE YOU LAUGH OUT LOUD

1. *Alice in Wonderland*, Lewis Carroll
2. *Chicana Falsa*, Michelle Serros
3. *The Complete Prose of Woody Allen*, Woody Allen
4. *The Diary of Adrian Mole, Aged 13 3/4*, Sue Townsend
5. *Heartburn*, Nora Ephron
6. *Operating Instructions: A Journal of My Son's First Year*, Annie Lamott
7. *Our Hearts Were Young and Gay*, Camelia O. Skinner and Emily Kimborough
8. *Portnoy's Complaint*, Philip Roth
9. *A Prayer for Owen Meany*, John Irving
10. *Seinlanguage*, Jerry Seinfeld

THE CULTURAL LITERACY LIST

1. *The Adventures of Huckleberry Finn*, Mark Twain
2. *Catcher in the Rye*, J. D. Salinger
3. *Death of a Salesman*, Arthur Miller
4. *The Diary of Anne Frank*
5. *Great Gatsby*, F. Scott Fitzgerald
6. *Hamlet*, William Shakespeare
7. *The Invisible Man*, Ralph Ellison
8. *The Odyssey*, Homer (Fagels translation)
9. *On the Road*, Jack Kerouac
10. *The Scarlet Letter*, Nathaniel Hawthorne

TEN BOOKS ABOUT LOVE

1. *Beloved*, Toni Morrison
2. *The English Patient*, Michael Ondaatje
3. *Like Water for Chocolate*, Laura Esquivel
4. *Little Altars Everywhere*, Rebecca Wells
5. *Love in the Time of Cholera*, Garbriel Garcia Marquez
6. *Love Medicine*, Louise Erdrich
7. *The Riders*, Tim Winton
8. *Snow Falling on Cedars*, David Guterson
9. *Summer of My German Soldier*, Bette Greene
10. *The Things They Carried*, Tim O'Brien

TEN BOOKS FOR A MAD, MAD, MAD WORLD

1. *Amphigorey*, by Edward Gorey
2. *Black Dahlia*, James Ellroy
3. *A Bright Red Scream: Self Mutilation and the Language of Pain*, Marilee Strong
4. *Brothers and Keepers*, John Edgar Wideman
5. *Dear America: Letters Home from Vietnam*,
   Bernard Edelman and Paul McCarthy (editors)
6. *Girl Interrupted*, Suzanne Kaysen
7. *Rule of the Bone*, Russell Banks
8. *The Stand*, Stephen King
9. *Trainspotting*, Irvine Welsh
10. *The World According to Garp*, John Irving

TEN BOOKS TO HELP TEACHERS SURVIVE MIDDLE
SCHOOL LANGUAGE ARTS

1. *After THE END*, Barry Lane
2. *Daybook of Critical Reading and Writing, 8th Grade Edition*, Fran Claggett,
   Louann Reid, Ruth Vinz
3. *The Dragon Apparent*, Louran Lewis

4. *Drawing Your Own Conclusions*, Fran Claggett and Joan Brown
5. *A Fine Young Man: What Parents, Mentors, and Educators Can Do to Shape Adolescent Boys into Exceptional Men*, Michael Gurian
6. *In the Middle, Second Edition*, Nancie Atwell
7. *School Girls*, Peggy Orenstein
8. *Seeking Diversity*, Linda Rief
9. *Words Their Way*, Donald Bear and Shane Templeton
10. *Writers in Training*, Rebekah Kaplan

TEN AUTHORS FOR MYSTERY LOVERS

1. James Lee Burke
2. Agatha Christie
3. Colin Dexter
4. Elizabeth George
5. Batya Gur
6. Tony Hillerman
7. P. D. James
8. John Lecarré
9. Walter Mosley
10. Jan Willem Van der Wetering

TEN NOBEL PRIZE WINNERS TO READ

1. Nadine Gordimer
2. Seamus Heaney
3. Gabriel Garcia Marquez
4. Ernest Hemingway
5. Eugene O'Neill
6. Czeslaw Milosz
7. Toni Morrison
8. Kenzaboro Oe
9. Wislawa Szymbosrska
10. W. B. Yeats

TEN BOOKS FOR THOSE IN PAIN OR DESPAIR

1. *Anything*, Dr. Seuss
2. *Bastard Out of Carolina*, Dorothy Allison
3. *The Book of Psalms*, The Bible
4. *Care of the Soul*, Thomas Moore
5. *Charlie and the Chocolate Factory*, Roald Dahl
6. *The Diving Bell and the Butterfly*, Jean-Dominique Bauby
7. *Feeling Good*, Dr. Burns
8. *How Stella Got Her Groove Back*, Terry McMillan
9. *Their Eyes Are Watching God*, Zora Neal Hurston
10. *Under the Eye of the Clock*, Christopher Nolan

TEN BOOKS FOR PARENTS

1. *Get Out of My Life, But First Could You Drive Me and Cheryl to the Mall?: A Parent's Guide to the New Teenager*, Anthony Wolf
2. *Letters from Dad: Lessons and Love*, John Broome and Jack Broome
3. *Lunchbox Love Notes: Notes for a Child (Love Notes)*, Gary Johnson
4. *Operating Instructions: A Journal of My Son's First Year*, Annie Lamott
5. *Raising a Daughter: Parents and the Awakening of a Healthy Woman*, Jeanne Elium and Don Elium
6. *Raising Lifelong Learners*, Lucy Calkins
7. *Raising a Son: Parents and the Making of a Healthy Man*, Don Elium and Jeanne Elium
8. *Reviving Ophelia: Saving the Selves of Adolescent Girls*, Mary Pipher
9. *Touchpoints*, T. Berry Brazelton
10. *The Wonder of Boys*, Michael Gurian

TEN BOOKS ABOUT FASCINATING PEOPLE

1. *An American Requiem: God, My Father, and the War that Came Between Us*, James Carroll
2. *The American Sphinx: The Character of Thomas Jefferson*, Joseph Ellis
3. *And the Band Played On*, Randy Shilts
4. *Daisy Bates in the Desert*, Julia Blackburn
5. *The Good Nazi: The Life and Lies of Albert Speer*, Dan Van Der Vat
6. *Life and Death in Shanghai*, Nien Cheng
7. *Mabel McKay: Weaving the Dream (Portraits of American Genius)*, Greg Sarris
8. *Nobody Nowhere*, Donna Williams
9. *Surely You're Joking, Mr. Feynman*, Richard Feynman
10. *Thirteen Ways of Looking at a Black Man*, Henry Louis Gates, Jr.

TEN BOOKS FOR THE PHILOSOPHICAL

1. *Cloister Walk*, Kathleen Norris
2. *Collected Fictions*, Jorge Luis Borges
3. *A History of Knowledge: Past, Present, and Future*, Charles Van Doren
4. *The Little Prince*, Antoine De Saint-Exupery
5. *Man's Search for Meaning*, Viktor Frankl
6. *Philosophical Investigations*, Phillip Kerr
7. *The Proper Study of Mankind: An Anthology of Essays*, Isaiah Berlin
8. *The Second Sex*, Simone de Beauvoir
9. *Six Great Ideas*, Mortimer Adler
10. *Sophie's World*, Jostein Gaardner

TEN BOOKS ABOUT PLACE

1. *An Area of Darkness*, V. S. Naipaul
2. *Balkan Ghosts: A Journey Through History*, Robert Kaplan
3. *Big Dreams: Into the Heart of California*, Bill Barich
4. *Dakota: A Spiritual Geography*, Kathleen Norris

5. *Labyrinth of Solitude,* Octavio Paz
6. *Lonesome Dove,* Larry McMurtry
7. *Midaq Alley,* Naghib Mafouz
8. *Patagonia,* Bruce Chatwin
9. *San Francisco Stories,* John Miller
10. *A Year in Province,* Peter Mayle

TEN POETS I COULD NOT LIVE WITHOUT

1. Lucille Clifton
2. Jack Gilbert
3. Li-Young Lee
4. Philip Levine
5. Antonio Machado
6. Czeslaw Milosz
7. Pablo Neruda
8. Ranier Maria Rilke
9. William Stafford
10. Wallace Stevens

TEN BOOKS TO TURN TO WHEN YOU ARE TRYING TO FORGET
THAT HUGE STACK OF ESSAYS DUE BACK ON MONDAY

1. *Anguished English,* Richard Lederer
2. *Charing Cross Road,* Helene Hanff
3. *Depth Takes a Holiday: Essays from Lesser Los Angeles,* Sandra Tsing Loh
4. *Essays That Worked,* Boykin Curry and Brian Kosbar
5. *Ex Libris: Confessions of a Common Reader,* Anne Fadiman
6. *It Was a Dark and Stormy Night,* Scott Rice
7. *Mother Tongue,* Bill Bryson
8. *Mrs. Fields Cookie Book,* Debbie Fields
9. *The Rants,* Dennis Miller
10. *Video Nights in Katmandu,* Pico Iyer

TEN BOOKS FOR THE TRAVELER

1. *Blue Highways,* William Least Heat Moon
2. *Longitude: The True Story of a Lone Genius Who Solved the Greatest Scientific Problem of His Time,* Dava Sobel
3. *On Persephone's Island (A Sicilian Journal),* Mary Taylor Simeti
4. *On the Road,* Jack Kerouac
5. *Riding the Iron Rooster: By Train Through China,* Paul Theroux
6. *Songlines,* Bruce Chatwin
7. *The Stones of Florence,* Mary McCarthy
8. *Transylvania and Beyond,* Devla Murphy
9. *Travelers' Tales: A Woman's World,* Marybeth Bond (editor)
10. *Under the Tuscan Sun: At Home in Italy,* Frances Mayes

TEN BOOKS FOR A RAINY DAY

1. *Babeltower*, A. S. Byatt
2. *Beach Music*, Pat Conroy
3. *Cold Mountain*, Charles Frazier
4. *Dear Theo: The Autobiography of Vincent Van Gogh*, Vincent Van Gogh (Irving and Jean Stone, editors)
5. *Gulliver's Travels*, Jonathan Swift
6. *Letters to a Young Poet*, Ranier Maria Rilke
7. *The Notebook*, Nicholas Sparks
8. *One Hundred Years of Solitude*, Gabriel Garcia Marquez
9. *Practical Magic*, Alice Hoffman
10. *The Rain God*, Arturo Islas

TEN BOOKS ABOUT READING

1. *Beginning to Read: Thinking and Learning about Print*, Marilyn Jager Adams
2. *Changing Our Minds: Negotiating English and Literacy*, Miles Myers
3. *I Hear America Reading: Why We Read • What We Read*, Jim Burke
4. *It's Never Too Late: Leading Adolescents to Lifelong Literacy*, Janet Allen
5. *The Literacy Crisis: False Claims, Real Solutions*, Jeff McQuillan
6. *Mosaic of Thought: Teaching Comprehension in a Reader's Workshop*, Ellin Oliver Keene and Susan Zimmerman
7. *The Read-Aloud Handbook*, Jim Trelease
8. *Reading Engagement: Motivating Readers Through Integrated Instruction*, John T. Guthrie and Alan Wigfield (editors)
9. *Reading Lessons*, Gerry Coles
10. *Reading Teacher's Book of Lists*, Edward Fry

TEN BOOKS YOU PLAN TO READ WHEN YOU RETIRE (BUT PROBABLY WON'T)

1. *The Bible*
2. *The Collected Dialogues of Plato*
3. *Finnegans Wake*, James Joyce
4. *Grapes of Wrath*, John Steinbeck
5. *Les Misérables*, Victor Hugo
6. *Moby Dick*, Herman Melville
7. *Remembrance of Things Past*, Marcel Proust
8. *The Rise and Fall of the Third Reich*, William L. Shirer
9. *Seven Pillars of Wisdom: A Triumph*, T. E. Lawrence
10. *War and Peace*, Leo Tolstoy

TEN BOOKS FOR THE RUGGED INDIVIDUALIST

1. *The Border Trilogy (All the Pretty Horses, The Crossing, Cities of the Plains)*, Cormac McCarthy
2. *China Men*, Maxine Hong Kingston
3. *Cowboys Are My Weakness*, Pam Houston

4. *Dalva,* Jim Harrison
5. *Even Cowgirls Get the Blues,* Tom Robbins
6. *Fountainhead,* Ayn Rand
7. *The Handmaid's Tale,* Margaret Atwood
8. *The Monkey Wrench Gang,* Edward Abbey
9. *Undaunted Courage,* Stephen Ambrose
10. *Walden,* Henry David Thoreau

TEN BOOKS FOR THE SCIENTIST IN US ALL

1. *Bully for Brontosaurus: Reflections in Natural History,* Stephen Jay Gould
2. *Composing a Life,* Mary Catherine Bateson
3. *Consilience: The Unity of Knowledge,* Edward O. Wilson
4. *Darwin's Dangerous Idea: Evolution and the Meanings of Life,* Daniel C. Dennett
5. *The Demon-Haunted World,* Carl Sagan
6. *Good Benito,* Alan Lightman
7. *The Hot Zone,* Richard Preston
8. *Lives of a Cell,* Lewis Thomas
9. *The Star Thrower,* Loren Eiseley
10. *The Turning Point,* Fritjof Capra

TEN BOOKS FOR THE SHORT STORY LOVER

1. *Arranged Marriage,* Chitna Banerjee Divakaruni
2. *The Collected Stories of Ernest Hemingway,* Ernest Hemingway
3. *The Collected Stories of Flannery O'Connor,* Flannery O'Connor
4. *The Collected Stories of John Cheever,* John Cheever
5. *Flash Fiction,* James Thomas
6. *Microfiction,* Jerome Stern (editor)
7. *Selected Stories,* Andrey Dubus
8. *The Vintage Contemporary Book of American Short Stories,*
   Tobias Wolff (editors)
9. *Where I'm Calling From,* Raymond Carver
10. *You've Got to Read This!,* Ron Hansen and Jim Shepherd (editors)

TEN BOOKS ABOUT TEACHING

1. *Bird by Bird,* Annie Lamott
2. *The Genesis of Ethics,* Burton Vysotski
3. *Letters of James Agee to Father Flye,* James Agee
4. *To Kill a Mockingbird,* Harper Lee
5. *A Lesson Before Dying,* Ernest Gaines
6. *Letters to Alice: On First Reading Jane Austen,* Fay Weldon
7. *The Measure of Our Success: A Letter to My Children and Yours,*
   Marian Wright Edelman
8. *Poetic Justice: The Literary Imagination and Public Life,* Martha Nussbaum
9. *Spitwad Sutras: Classroom Teaching as Sublime Vocation,* Robert Inchausti
10. *Zen and the Art of Motorcycle Maintenance,* Robert Pirsig

TEN BOOKS FOR SPORTS FANS

1. *Hard Courts: Real Life on the Professional Tennis Tours,* John Feinstein
2. *In These Girls the Heart Is a Muscle,* Madeleine Blais
3. *Little Girls in Pretty Boxes,* Joan Ryan
4. *Once More Around the Park: A Baseball Reader,* Roger Angell
5. *Sacred Hoops: Spiritual Lessons of a Hardwood Warrior,*
   Phil Jackson (and Hugh Delehanty)
6. *A Season on the Brink: A Season with Bob Knight and the Indiana Hoosiers,*
   John Feinstein
7. *Stoked: A History of Surf Culture,* Drew Kampion and Bruce Brown
8. *The Thinking Man's Guide to Professional Football,* Paul Zimmerman
9. *Values of the Game,* Bill Bradley
10. *Winterdance: The Fine Madness of Running the Iditarod,* Gary Paulsen

TEN BOOKS IN SEARCH OF THE TRUTH

1. *Alburquerque,* Rudolfo Ananya
2. *The Discoverers: A History of Man's Search to Know His World and Himself,*
   Daniel J. Boorstin
3. *Fragments: Memories of a Wartime Childhood,* Binjamin Wilkomirski
4. *Full House: The Spread of Excellence from Plato to Darwin,* Stephen Jay Gould
5. *The Meaning of It All: Thoughts of a Citizen Scientist,* Richard Feynman
6. *Notes of a Native Son,* James Baldwin
7. *The Rape of Nanking: The Forgotten Holocaust,* Iris Chang
8. *Seeing Voices: A Journey into the World of the Deaf,* Oliver Sacks
9. *Serpico,* Frank Serpico
10. *Sophie's Choice,* William Styron

Appendix B

A Brief Directory of Useful Literacy Resources

This is not meant to be an exhaustive list of all available resources. Instead, I have tried to include some essential organizations that should, through their Web sites, provide you access to still other, more specific web sites that might be of interest. Further resources can be found on this book's companion Web site (www.englishcompanion.com).

American Library Association (ALA)

50 East Huron Street
Chicago, IL 60611
(312) 280-2162
URL: http://www.ala.org/

The ALA provides a wealth of resources through their Web site, including reviews, awards, recommended books, and tips to help readers of all ages.

Books and Beyond

309 North Rios Avenue
Solana Beach, CA 92075
(619) 755-3823
E-mail: booksbey@sbsd.k12.ca.us
URL: http://www.sbsd.k12.ca.us/sbsd/specialprog/BB/

This program offers a powerful example of investment in literacy, one that has become a model to other communities. The Web site includes practical solutions and helpful resources. A dynamic group of people leads the program and have much to teach and share.

Carol Hurst's Children's Literature Site

URL: http://www.carolhurst.com/

Teachers and librarians will appreciate this rich collection of reviews, curriculum ideas, and activities. Reviews are organized by title, author, type of book, and grade level, and educators can also look for ideas based on curriculum areas or themes. There's plenty here to help educators integrate literature into their curriculum.

The Center for the Book

Library of Congress
101 Independence Avenue, SE
Washington, DC 20540-4920
(202) 707-5221
URL: http://lcweb.loc.gov/loc/cfbook/

The Center for the Book, created by Congress in 1977, was established to stimulate public interest in books, reading, and libraries, and to encourage the study of books and print culture. Working through an expanding network of affiliated centers throughout the country, the Center sponsors and offers a wide variety of programs to help achieve its goal of increased literacy and appreciation for the printed word. Its Web site offers very interesting resources, publications, and information to all who are interested in books.

Center for the Improvement of Early Reading Achievement (CIERA)

University of Michigan School of Education
610 E. University Avenue, Rm. 1600 SEB
Ann Arbor, MI 48109-1259
(734) 647-6940
URL: http://www.ciera.org/

CIERA's mission is to improve the reading ability of all children. Its staff strives to accomplish this through many research studies, publications, and helpful, practical solutions, all of which can be accessed through their excellect Web site.

Children's Literature Web Guide

URL: http://www.acs.ucalgary.ca/~dkbrown/

A remarkable site that exemplifies how well and how much a Web site can gather and organize a wide range of resources to help professionals. This site includes extensive book lists, lists of award winners, and practical reading suggestions for individuals and programs. (It clocked 500,000 visits in its first six months.)

Helping Your Child Learn to Read

URL: http://www.ed.gov/pubs/parents/Reading/index.html

This U. S. Department of Education online resource by Bernice Cullinan and Brod Bagert provides tips and activities to promote reading for children from infancy through age ten.

International Reading Association (IRA)

800 Barksdale Road
P. O. Box 8139
Newark, DE 19714-8139
(800) 336-7223
URL: http://www.ira.org/

IRA, through its excellent Web site and many publications, offers some of the best resources and support for teachers, schools, or programs trying to expand and improve literacy. The group publishes several journals that focus on different aspects of literacy (e.g., adult, early childhood, research).

Literacy Volunteers of America, Inc. (LVA)

635 James Street
Syracuse, NY 13203-2214
(800) 582-8812
E-mail: lvanat@aol.com
URL: http://www.literacyvolunteers.org/

Literacy Volunteers of America, Inc. (LVA) is a national network committed to changing lives through literacy. Professionally trained volunteer tutors teach Basic Literacy and English for Speakers of Other Languages. Literacy skills enable LVA students to be better parents, workers, and citizens. The group makes a conscious effort to address the needs of family literacy, technology in literacy, and those with learning difficulties.

Maureen's Read-Aloud Page

URL: http://www.bhs.edu/wmc/mis/readaloud.html

This site is designed for parents and teachers who want to help teach children how to read and to love reading. It offers practical advice about what to do and how to do it, focusing specifically on the benefits of reading aloud.

National Clearinghouse for ESL Literacy Education (NCLE)

4646 40th Street, NW
Washington, DC 20016-1859
(202) 362-0700, ext. 200
E-mail: ncle@cal.org
URL: http://www.cal.org/ncle/

This Web site offers excellent access to publications and strategies for helping English Language Learners develop their literacy skills.

National Institute for Literacy (NIFL)

Literacy Information and Communication System (LINCS)
URL: http://novel.nifl.gov/

LINCS is a cooperative electronic network of the National Institute for Literacy that strives to bring all adult literacy-related resources, expertise, and knowledge to a single focal point. The coordinated efforts of NIFL's national LINCS, LINCS regional partners, and participating states have made LINCS America's only national information retrieval and communication system for literacy.

Reading Is Fundamental (RIF)

600 Maryland Avenue, SW Suite 600
Washington, DC 20024
(202) 287-3220
URL: http://www.rif.org/

Reading Is Fundamental is America's leading nonprofit children's literacy organization. Through a network of volunteer-run programs, RIF gets free books into kids' hands and makes reading fun through exciting reading-related activities. RIF believes the best way to help children discover the joy of reading—and become lifelong readers—is to involve them in reading early and often. Since literacy begins at home, RIF helps parents make reading a family priority and involves them in their children's reading and learning through programs and materials.

Rolling Readers USA

3049 University Avenue
San Diego, CA 92104
800-390-7323 or (619) 296-4095
To find your local chapter: (800) 390-7323
E-mail: rollread@cts.com

A wonderful organization that links community partners with elementary-age readers who need more individualized attention. A proven organizational and instructional model, Rolling Readers has plenty to teach the program or the tutor.

Student Coalition for Action in Literacy Education (SCALE)

140 1/2 East Franklin Street
CB#3505 UNC-CH
Chapel Hill, NC 27599-3505
(919) 962-1542
E-mail : scale@unc.edu
URL: http://www.unc.edu/depts/scale/

SCALE is a national organization that mobilizes college students to address this country's literacy needs through partnership with community agencies, service organizations, new readers, students, faculty, and administrators.

Tales of Wonder

URL: http://darsie.ucdavis.edu/tales/

This elegant Web site, which offers folk and fairy tales from around the world, is a model of the care that makes a great online resource. Larger font sizes and varied text/background colors for the stories, good categorization, and an ample supply of tales from many different cultures and regions make this a page that could support a whole unit on world folk tales.

Tips on Tutoring

URL: http://www.sfsv.org/tutor.html

These useful, if somewhat predictable, tips appear on San Francisco School Volunteers' Web site, which offers insight into how an exemplary local organization can make a real difference in education.

United States Department of Education (DOE)

600 Independence Avenue, SW, Room 6100
Washington, DC 20202
(800) USA-LEARN
(800) 437-0833 (TDD)

URL: http://www.ed.gov/
URL: http://www.ed.gov/inits/americareads/

The DOE Web site offers abundant resources for individuals and programs. This site also provides information about the government's America Reads program and regional centers of the national literacy program.

Western/Pacific Literacy Network

State Literacy Resource Center of California
1086 Eighth Street
Oakland, CA 94607
(510) 834-7835
E-mail: pheaven@literacynet.org
URL: http://literacynet.org

This outstanding site provides a wealth of links, resources, and helpful ideas for individuals and programs.

APPENDIX C

Hooked on Fish

BY CAROL JAGO

While browsing my junk mail, I happened upon the Santa Monica Seafood newsletter. It is hard to say why this particular article caught my eye, but I found myself reading an article from the National Fisheries Institute about getting children to eat fish. The more I read the more I kept finding similarities between their advice and what I think works for getting small children hooked on books.

1. "If you normally eat fish twice a month, increase to three times a month, then once a week and so on."

If you normally read to your child at bedtime, try finding other times during the day to pick up a book together. Reading should not be relegated to those moments when both of you are most tired. Carry picture books in your car, bring them into restaurants, keep a pile in the bathroom. The greater children's exposure to books, even before they can read, the easier learning to read will be for them.

2. "Serve fish with other foods your children enjoy, like spaghetti or mashed potatoes."

If you know your child loves trucks or cats or worms or ice cream, look for books about them. A child's attitude toward reading will be influenced by attraction to the subject. It is a way to prime the literacy well. Many children who say they don't like reading have never found a book they like. Make it your mission to keep this from happening. Try both fiction and nonfiction texts. Boys particularly often prefer "true" stories.

3. "Introduce only one new food per meal."

Small children typically find a favorite book, for example *Goodnight, Moon*, *Where the Wild Things Are*, or *Bedtime for Frances* and ask for it to be read to the exclusion of all others. Continue rereading these old familiars (who knows what literary pleasure centers those particular words are touching), but introduce new stories as well, one per session. Don't let it bother you if some of these new titles fall flat. Who hasn't picked up books they hated? Use your public library. Only buy once you know you have found a winner.

4. "Let children help prepare the meal."

Visit the library or your local bookstore together. Discuss the kinds of books you are looking for. Talk about how you choose a book out of the many available. Then let children choose on their own. Give children a book allowance along with their other pocket money. Have your child mark the date when library books are due.

5. "Try the 'one-bite' method. If they don't like it, let them remove the bite and praise them for trying the fish."

Read aloud passages from the book you are yourself reading. Share your favorite poetry even if you know it is far beyond your child's ken. There is a magic to words that work upon the reader in ways that go past simple comprehension. But if the child is bored, stop. Thank him or her for trying to listen, and try again in another six months.

The National Fisheries Institute conclusion was apt. "Don't be discouraged if your kids don't flip over the fish you prepare. It often takes several experiences with a new food for them to accept it, and several more before they'll like it." The same is true for helping children partake of literature. At first it may not wow them, but over time it will. I promise you it will.

Carol Jago teaches English at Santa Monica High School and directs the California Reading and Literature Project at UCLA. "Hooked on Fish" was a letter to the editor in Education Week.